D0423178

Language and Language Learning

A LINGUISTIC THEORY
OF TRANSLATION

Language and Language Learning

General Editors: R. MACKIN and P. D. STREVENS

1   Henry Sweet: *The Practical Study of Languages*
2   J. R. Firth: *The Tongues of Men* and *Speech*
3   Randolph Quirk and A. H. Smith: *The Teaching of English*
4   Neile Osman: *Modern English*
5   Harold E. Palmer: *The Principles of Language Study*
6   N. E. Enkvist, J. Spencer and M. Gregory: *Linguistics and Style*
7   Harold E. Palmer: *Curso Internacional de Inglés*
8   J. C. Catford: *A Linguistic Theory of Translation*
9   P. D. Strevens: *Papers in Language and Language Teaching*
10 D. Abercrombie: *Studies in Phonetics and Linguistics*

A Linguistic Theory
of Translation

An Essay in Applied Linguistics

J. C. CATFORD

LONDON
Oxford University Press
1965

Oxford University Press, Amen House, London E.C.4

GLASGOW   NEW YORK   TORONTO   MELBOURNE   WELLINGTON
BOMBAY   CALCUTTA   MADRAS   KARACHI   LAHORE   DACCA
CAPE TOWN   SALISBURY   NAIROBI   IBADAN   ACCRA
KUALA LUMPUR   HONG KONG

© *Oxford University Press, 1965*

P
3 06
- C 3 3

PRINTED AND BOUND IN ENGLAND BY
HAZELL WATSON AND VINEY LTD
AYLESBURY, BUCKS

Contents

CHAPTER   PAGE

1   General Linguistic Theory   1

2   Translation: Definition and General Types   20

3   Translation Equivalence   27

4   Formal Correspondence   32

5   Meaning and Total Translation   35

6   Transference   43

7   Conditions of Translation Equivalence   49

8   Phonological Translation   56

9   Graphological Translation   62

10   Transliteration   66

11   Grammatical and Lexical Translation   71

12   Translation Shifts   73

13   Language Varieties in Transiation   83

14   The Limits of Translatability   93

141461

Preface

TRANSLATION is an activity of enormous importance in the modern world and it is a subject of interest not only to linguists, professional and amateur translators and language-teachers, but also to electronic engineers and mathematicians. Books and articles on translation have been written by specialists in all these fields. Writers on the subject have approached it from different points of view—regarding translation as a literary art, or as a problem in computer-programming, discussing the problem of 'faithfulness' of rendering, of whether words or 'ideas' are to be translated, or of the routines to be set up, say, for stem and affix recognition in machine translation.

The present volume is not primarily concerned with any of these special problems, but rather with the analysis of what translation *is*. It proposes general categories to which we can assign our observations of particular instances of translation, and it shows how these categories relate to one another. In short, it sets up, though somewhat tentatively and incompletely, a theory of translation which may be drawn upon in any discussion of particular translation-problems.

Since translation has to do with language, the analysis and description of translation-processes must make considerable use of categories set up for the description of languages. It must, in other words, draw upon a theory of language—a general linguistic theory.

This book is based on lectures given in the School of Applied Linguistics at Edinburgh University. It was thus originally intended for an audience of students already fairly well-informed about general linguistics. To make it more acceptable to the general reader, an opening chapter has been added which discusses briefly the nature of language and the categories of general linguistics as well as giving an outline of the analysis and description of English which underlies the discussion of a number of examples. Parts of the book are somewhat technical. This is inevitable in a book on a specialized topic, but it should not dismay the general reader since the main arguments demand little or no previous knowledge of linguistic science and the first chapter may be used for reference when required.

Language-teachers, in particular, may find the book of interest. The extent to which translation can be used in language-teaching is an issue of great concern to teachers, and it is one which cannot be fruitfully discussed without the support of some theory about what translation is, about the nature of translation equivalence, the difference between translation equivalence and formal correspondence, the levels of language at which translations may be performed and so on. The chief defect of the now almost universally condemned 'Grammar-Translation Method' was that it used bad grammar and bad translation—translation is not a dangerous technique in itself provided its nature is understood, and its use is carefully controlled: and translation is in itself a valuable skill to be imparted to students.

A number of students and colleagues contributed useful suggestions when the essay was first circulated in duplicated draft form, to all of whom I am grateful. In particular, however, I should like to thank Dr M. A. K. Halliday, with whom I discussed many parts of the work while it was in preparation, and Miss Leila Dixon, who carried out the difficult task of typing the manuscript in several stages.

J. C. Catford

Edinburgh, 1964

1

General Linguistic Theory

1.0   Translation is an operation performed on languages: a process of substituting a text in one language for a text in another. Clearly, then, any theory of translation must draw upon a theory of language—a general linguistic theory.

General Linguistics is, primarily, a theory about how languages work. It provides categories, drawn from generalizations based on observation of languages and language-events. These categories can, in turn, be used in the description of any particular language. The general linguistic theory made use of in this book is essentially that developed at the University of Edinburgh, in particular by M. A. K. Halliday[1] and influenced to a large extent by the work of the late J. R. Firth. The present writer, however, takes full responsibility for the brief and, indeed, oversimplified sketch of linguistic theory given here, which differs from that of Halliday chiefly in its treatment of *levels* (1.2).

1.1   Our starting-point is a consideration of how language is related to the human social situations in which it operates. This leads on to classification of *levels* of language (or of linguistic analysis) and then to a discussion of the fundamental *categories* of linguistics which can be used in the description of at least the grammar and phonology of particular languages.

Language is a type of patterned human behaviour. It is a way, perhaps the most important way, in which human beings interact in social situations. Language-behaviour is externalized or manifested in some kind of bodily activity on the part of a *performer*, and presupposes the existence of at least one other human participant in the situation, an *addressee*.[2]

---

[1] For a fuller account than it is possible to give here, the reader is referred to M. A. K. Halliday, 'Categories of the Theory of Grammar', *Word*, Vol. 17, No. 3, 1961, pp. 241–92; also to Halliday, M. A. K., McIntosh, A., and Strevens, P. D. 'The Linguistic Sciences and Language Teaching'. Longmans, 1964.

[2] *Performer* and *addressee* are 'participant rôles'. In the limiting case of a man talking to himself—i.e. interacting linguistically with himself—both rôles are

The specific type of behaviour in which language is manifested not only identifies the behaviour *as* language-behaviour but also defines the *medium* which the performer is using. The performer's activity most commonly takes the form of either vocal movements which generate sound-waves, or hand movements which leave a visible trace. The first type of activity is a manifestation of language in the *spoken* medium—the performer is a speaker, and his addressee(s) is/are a hearer or hearers. The second type is a manifestation of language in the *written* medium—the performer is a writer, and his addressee(s) is/are a reader or readers. In the next paragraph we shall, for simplicity, confine ourselves to language in its spoken manifestation.

Language, as we said above, is *patterned* behaviour. It is, indeed, the pattern which *is* the language. On any given occasion, the particular vocal movements and the resultant sound-waves can be described with a *delicacy*, or depth of detail, limited only by the delicacy of the apparatus used for observation and analysis. And the precise quality of these vocal movements and sound-waves will be found to differ on different occasions, even when the speaker is 'saying the same thing'. From the linguistic point of view, the important thing is that, on each occasion of 'saying the same thing' the vocal activities of the speaker conform to the same pattern.

The overt language-behaviour described above is causally related to various other features of the situation in which it occurs. There are specific objects, events, relations and so on, in the situation, which lead the performer to produce these particular vocal movements, and no others. The precise nature of the situational features which are relatable to the performer's linguistic behaviour will be found to differ on different occasions, even when he is 'saying the same thing'.

From the linguistic point of view, however, the important thing again is that, in each case, the situational features which lead to 'the same' utterance conform to the same general pattern.

Language then is an activity which may be said to impinge on the world at large at two ends. On the one hand, it is *manifested*

filled simultaneously by the same biological individual: but this is of the most marginal relevance to linguistic theory (cf. 13.2).

in specific kinds of overt behaviour (e.g. vocal movements): on the other hand, it is *related* to specific objects, events, etc. in the situation. Both of these—vocal movements, and actual events, etc.—are outside of language itself. They are extralinguistic events. They are the *phonic substance* in which vocal activity is manifested, and the *situation* (or *situation substance*) to which this activity is related. The language itself is, however, the organization or patterning which language-behaviour implicitly imposes on these two kinds of substance—language is *form*, not substance.

1.2   In order to account for language-events we make abstractions from these events: abstractions of various types, or at a series of *levels*.

1.21   We distinguish, first, the levels of *medium-substance* (*phonic* substance, for the spoken medium, and *graphic* substance for the written medium), and *situation* (or *situation-substance*), both of which are, in fact, extralinguistic. The internal levels of *language* are those of medium-form—*phonology* and *graphology*, arrived at by a process of abstraction from phonic and graphic substance, and the differently abstracted levels, which Halliday calls the 'formal levels'—*grammar* and *lexis*.[3]

The relationship between (the units of) grammar/lexis and situation (substance) is that of contextual meaning, or *context*.

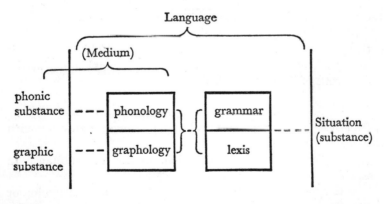

---

[3] The term 'formal levels' for grammar and lexis has the inconvenience that it suggests that no relatively independent *form* can be stated for the phonological and graphological levels.

The relationship between (the units of) phonology and phonic substance has no generally recognized name, though 'phonetic meaning' might be suggested. The relationship between graphology and graphic substance might likewise be called 'graphetic meaning'. *Context* is an important *interlevel* and is included in the diagram above, which indicates the relationship between the various levels.

1.22   The levels at which we make abstractions from language-events are thus the following:

1.221   *Grammatical/lexical form*

(i) *Grammar:* the level of linguistic form at which operate *closed systems*: the characteristics of a closed system being: (1) the number of terms is finite; (2) each term is exclusive of the others; (3) any change in the number of terms would change the 'values' (or 'formal meanings') of the other terms (e.g. systems of pronouns, of deictics, of number, of case, of tense . . . etc.).

(ii) *Lexis:* the level of linguistic form at which operate *open sets* (e.g. the open sets of items often occurring as examples or 'exponents' of nouns, verbs, etc.).

1.222   *Medium form*

(i) *Phonology:* the formal units into which phonic substance is organized, and which operate, usually in combination, as the exponents of grammatical/lexical forms.

(ii) *Graphology:* the formal units into which graphic substance is organized, and which operate, usually in combination, as the exponents of grammatical/lexical forms.

1.223   *Medium Substance*

(i) *Phonic substance:* actual vocal sounds—the substance in which phonology is manifested.

(ii) *Graphic substance:* actual visible marks—the substance in which graphology is manifested.

Both types of medium substance have a certain patterning or organization imposed upon them by medium-form.

1.224   *Situation* (or *situation substance*). All those features of situations, excluding medium substance, which are related or relatable to language-behaviour. Situation substance has a certain organization imposed upon it by grammatical/lexical form.

1.23   In addition, we must consider the *interlevel* of *context* (or *contextual meaning*): the interlevel of statements about the distinctive features of situation-substance which are relatable to particular grammatical/lexical forms. As we have said above, there is another *interlevel*: the interlevel of statements about the distinctive features of medium substance which are relatable to medium forms.

It will be clear that *context* or *contextual meaning* is what is most usually understood by 'meaning': in our theory, this is only one part of *meaning*, which also includes *formal meaning* which is the way any item operates in the network of formal relations. Both types of meaning are discussed in Chapter 5.

1.3   The fundamental categories of linguistic theory—applicable at least to the levels of grammar, phonology and probably graphology—are *unit*, *structure*, *class* and *system*.

1.31   By a *unit* we mean a stretch of language activity which is the carrier of a pattern of a particular kind. In English phonology, for example, there is a unit, the *tone-group*, which is the carrier of recurrent meaningful patterns of pitch. The following are examples of English tone-groups (the pitch-pattern being roughly indicated by lines drawn over the texts).

Yes.   Yesterday.   John came yesterday.

The fact that each of these tone-groups is a carrier of a *meaningful* pattern is shown by the possibility of occurrence of units of a similar type which differ only in that the pitch-pattern which they carry is meaningfully different, thus:

Yes?   Yesterday?   John came yesterday?

In English grammar we have units such as *sentence*, *clause* and *group*: each of these is the carrier of a particular kind of meaningful grammatical pattern. The following are examples of *sentences*, each carrying the same pattern of arrangement of clauses.

/// If you do that, // you will regret it. ///

/// When John arrived, // we had already started. ///

/// Having arrived too late, // we missed the start of the concert. ///

And these are examples of clauses, each carrying the same pattern of arrangement of groups:

// John / loves / Mary. //

// The young man / was writing / a letter. //

// All these people who were here last night / were / friends of mine. //

1.311   The units of grammar or of phonology operate in *hierarchies*—'larger' or more inclusive units being made up of 'smaller' or less inclusive units. They form a *scale* of units at different *ranks*. Thus, the sentences quoted above each consist of *two clauses*. The sentence is a unit of *higher rank* than the clause. And each clause consists of several *groups*—the clause being a unit of higher rank than the group.

1.32   The unit is the category set up to account for those stretches of language-activity which carry recurrent meaningful patterns. The patterns themselves still have to be accounted for —and these are what we call *structures*. A *structure* is an arrangement of *elements*. Thus, the elements of structure of the English unit 'clause' are P (predicator), S (subject), C (complement), A (adjunct).

The texts: /// John / loves / Mary. ///

/// The young man / was writing / a letter. ///

are two examples of English sentences, each of which consists of a single clause. Each clause has the *structure* SPC. The following clauses:

He / ran / quickly.

The young man / was writing / with a ball-point.

are examples of the structure SPA, and so on.

Among the units of English phonology we find the *syllable*: the elements of syllable structure are N (nucleus or vocalic element), K^r (releasing (initial) consonantal element), K^a (arresting consonantal element), K^i ('interlude' or inter-nuclear consonantal element—occurring only between two Ns). Thus the syllables represented in orthography by *tea, car, now* exemplify the structure KN, those represented by *cat, stop, lumps,* etc. . . . KNK, and so on.

1.33   By a *class* we mean a grouping of members of a unit in terms of the way in which they operate in the structure of the unit next above in the rank scale. Structure, as we have said, is stated in terms of ordered arrangements (in which linear *sequence* often is, but need not always be, a characteristic) of elements: thus, in English, the elements of structure of the unit *clause* are S, P, C, A. The units which operate as exponents of these elements are themselves *groups*. Groups, then, may be classified in terms of the particular elements of clause structure which they expound. Thus we have, in English, the class of *Verbal Groups*, which operate at—or as exponents of—P in clause-structure; the class of *Nominal Groups* which operate as exponents of S or C in clause-structure, etc.

In English phonology, for instance, we have classes of the unit *phoneme*, defined in terms of their operation in the structure of the unit next above, the *syllable*. Thus the members of the unit 'phoneme', which operate as exponents of the element K^r (consonantal releasing element) in syllable structure constitute the class 'initial consonant' or C^i.

1.34   By a *system* we mean a finite set of alternants, among which a choice must be made. Very often, these alternants, the *terms* in a system, are the members of a class: thus the members of the class 'initial consonant' mentioned above constitute a *system* of phonemes *p b t d k g* . . . etc. which can alternate as exponents of that particular class.

An example of a system in grammar might be the *number-system* (Sing/Plur) (Sing/Dual/Plural), etc., of many languages. Where *number* is a system of the Nominal group (as in English) the terms in the system are themselves sub-groups or sub-classes of the *class*.

1.4   We have referred already to *rank* (in 1.311) and have used the terms *exponent* and *delicacy*. These three terms refer to three *scales* which are part of the general theory of language, and of language-description.

1.41   The *rank scale* is the scale on which units are arranged in a grammatical or phonological hierarchy. In English grammar we set up a hierarchy of 5 units—the largest, or 'highest', on the rank-scale is the *sentence*. The smallest, or 'lowest', on the rank scale is the *morpheme*. Between these, in 'descending' order, are the *clause*, the *group* and the *word*. By placing these in this order on the scale of rank we mean that every sentence consists of one or more than one clause, every clause of one or more than one group, every group of one or more than one word, and every word of one or more than one morpheme.

Thus 'Yes!' is a sentence consisting of one clause, consisting of one group, consisting of one word, consisting of one morpheme. And 'As soon as the boys had arrived, their mother gave them tea'. is a sentence consisting of two clauses. The first clause consists of three groups, the second of four groups. In the first clause the group *as soon as* consists of three words, the groups *the boys* and *had arrived* of two words each. In the second clause, the first group *their mother* consists of two words, the remaining three groups of one word each . . . and so on.

1.411   The normal relation between units in a grammatical hierarchy is that stated here: namely that a unit at any rank consists of one or more unit of the rank next below, or, conversely, that a unit at any rank *operates in the structure of the unit next above*.

We must, however, make allowance for the fact that in all languages we find 'Chinese box' arrangements of units, in which a unit may sometimes operate in the structure of a unit of the *same* or of *lower* rank. To deal with this, we make use of the concept of *rank-shift*.

Thus, in English, *clauses* normally operate as exponents of elements of *sentence-structure*. But we also find clauses operating within *groups*, i.e. as exponents of elements in the structure of a unit of the rank *below* the clause.

For example, in *Since we couldn't meet earlier, we met after the concert* the clause *we met after the concert* is operating directly in the structure of the sentence, as exponent, in fact, of α (a 'free clause') in a sentence of structure βα (a 'free clause' preceded by a 'bound clause') (see 1.721 below). But in *The man we met after the concert is my brother* the clause *we met after the concert* is *rank-shifted*. It is not operating directly in the structure of the sentence, but within a Nominal Group. It is, in fact, operating as exponent of Q (qualifier) in the structure of the nominal group *The man we met after the concert*. This nominal group, in turn, is exponent of S in the clause *The man we met after the concert* (S) / *is* (P) / *my brother* (C).

Similarly in *He met Susan at the party* the adverbial group *at the party* is operating directly in the structure of the clause—as exponent of A. But in *The girl at the party was Susan* the group *at the party* is *rank-shifted*. It is not operating directly in the clause, but within a Nominal Group, as exponent of Q.

The concept of *rank* (and rank scale) is an important one both in theoretical linguistics and in many applications of linguistics, including translation-theory.

1.42   The scale of *exponence* is a scale of 'exemplification' or of degrees of abstraction, running from 'highest degree of abstraction' to 'most specific and concrete exemplification'. Thus, in English phonology, we may say that the class C (consonant) represents the highest degree of abstraction at phoneme rank. In any given instance, say of an utterance of the word *tea*, we may say that the initial phoneme here is a (member of the class) C: its exponent in this case is the particular phoneme / t /, and this, in turn, has its ultimate exponent in a piece of actual phonic substance, represented in phonetic transcription by, say, [t^h].

Exponence is related to rank in the sense that an element of structure of a unit at one rank is *expounded* by—or has as its exponent—a unit or units of the rank next below. But exponence is a separate scale, and at any one rank we may go off sideways, as it were, to a relatively concrete exemplification: thus we might call the sequence of particular grammatical and lexical items represented by 'A linguistic theory of translation' an *exponent* of the unit 'group'. In other words, we also use the term *exponent* in talking of the relationship between the abstract units and items of grammar and lexis and their realizations in medium form. Thus, in English, *I* is the graphological exponent of the grammatical item '1st person singular subject pronoun', *bank* is the graphological exponent of two different lexical items which we might label X (meaning 'money shop') and Y (meaning 'border of river . . . etc.') and so on.

1.43   The third scale mentioned here is that of *delicacy*: this is the scale of 'depth of detail'. At a *primary degree* of delicacy, we recognize, or set up, only the minimal number of units or classes, etc., which are forced upon us by the data. Thus, if we are going to attribute *any* structure at all to English *nominal groups* we must set up *three* elements: H (head), M (modifier) and Q (qualifier). Our *least delicate* description of English Ngp structure is thus (M . . . n) H (Q . . . n), which means that one element, H, is always present, and this may be preceded and/or followed by one or more element M or Q. Thus we should say, at a primary degree of delicacy, that the groups:

Old / men

These three old / men

have the structure, MH and MMMH. By taking a further step down the delicacy scale we recognize different classes of the element M — namely d (deictic), o (numerative), e (epithet), and we can say that *These three old / men* has the structure d o e H, in which d o e is a more delicate statement of structure than MMM.

1.5   *Lexis*. We stated in 1.221 that *lexis* is that part of language which is not describable in terms of closed systems. The distinction between grammar and lexis is not absolute, but rather in the nature of a *cline*, with very well marked poles, but some overlap in between.

In English, for instance, most exponents of the word-class *verb* are open-set lexical items: a few, such as *can, may* etc. are purely grammatical items: and a few others are either lexical or grammatical, e.g. BE which is a lexical item in 'He *is* a teacher' or 'He has *been* a teacher.' and a grammatical item in 'He *is* talking'.

1.51   The categories discussed in 1.2 are not applicable to lexis. We deal formally with lexis in terms of *collocation* and *lexical sets*. A collocation is the 'lexical company' that a particular lexical item keeps. Any particular lexical item tends to collocate most frequently with a range of other lexical items. We refer to the item under discussion as the *node* or *nodal item*, and the items with which it collocates as its *collocates*. Thus in English, if we take *sheep* and *mutton* as *nodes* we will find that each has a distinct range of *collocates*: e.g. *sheep* collocates frequently with such lexical items as *field, flock, shear*, etc., *mutton* collocates with such lexical items as *roast, menu, fat* . . . etc. There are certainly overlaps in collocational range—thus we may have *a (whole) roast sheep* and we might have *fat sheep* as well as *mutton fat*, but on the whole they have different collocational ranges, and this establishes the fact that they belong to different lexical sets and are different lexical items.

A *lexical set* is a group of lexical items which have similar collocational ranges.

1.52   *Collocation* and *lexical set* are concepts which sometimes enable us to establish the existence of two distinct lexical items, even when both share exactly the same medium exponents. Thus in English we have a graphological form *bank*—but the fact that this enters into two distinct collocational ranges, and hence apparently belongs to two distinct lexical sets enables us to say that there are two distinct lexical items which happen to share the same medium exponents, graphological *bank*, phonological / baŋk /.[4]

1.6   We mentioned in 1.0 that our approach to the *levels* of language and linguistic analysis was somewhat different from that of Halliday, and indicated in 1.21 that this difference lay in the fact that we set up a separate level of *medium form*. In other words, instead of regarding *phonology* (and likewise *graphology*) as an *interlevel* linking phonic (or graphic) substance directly with the 'formal levels' of grammar and lexis, we regard the *medium* as being to some extent autonomous and detachable from grammar and lexis. Since this view of medium as 'detachable' is important for our theory of translation, some justification and discussion of it must be given here.

1.61   Medium form is a part of a language. Every language has its characteristic *phonology* and many languages have a characteristic *graphology*. In the process of analysing and describing a language we set up, as phonological units, just those bundles of

---

[4] Following a widely accepted convention, phonological forms are normally cited within slant-lines. Occasional use is, however, made of single and double vertical lines, as in 1.61 below. These are used only when explicit reference is being made to the description of English Phonology given in 1.71.

distinctive phonic features which function contrastively in the exponence of grammatical and lexical items of that language. Thus we set up / p / and / b / as distinct phonemes because such pairs as / pig / and / big /, / pak / and / bak / are exponents of distinct lexical items: and we set up the *foot* or rhythmic unit as a phonological unit because the difference in foot-division between such pairs as

$$\| \text{ that's a } | \text{ blackbird } \|$$
$$\text{and } \| \text{ That's a } | \text{ black } | \text{ bird } \|$$

is exponent of a difference in grammatical structure:

| blackbird | = compound-noun as H in Ngp structure,
| black | bird | = adjective + noun as MH in Ngp structure.

1.62   In other words, the *discovery* procedure for phonological analysis must depend directly on grammatical/lexical differences. But once the phonology has been *established*, by discovering what phonic distinctions operate as exponents of grammatical/lexical distinctions in that particular language, it can be regarded—indeed must be regarded—as relatively autonomous or independent. It is this autonomy of phonology which makes it possible for two or more lexical or grammatical items to *share* the same phonological exponents—e.g. the three or more distinct English lexical items which share the one phonological exponent / piə /—partially distinguished in graphological exponence as *peer* and *pier*. It also makes it possible for one single item to have more than one phonological exponent, such as the English 'indefinite article' which has the alternative phonological exponents / ə / or / ən /, and the 'nominal plural morpheme' which has a series of phonological exponents / s,z,iz /, / ən /, / internal vowel-change / etc.

1.63   More striking evidence of the autonomy and detachability of *medium* is the fact that the grammar and lexis of *one* language can be expounded (though often with some losses in distinctiveness) in the *medium* of another. We are all familiar with the Englishmen who speaks French fluently and 'correctly', but who speaks it entirely through the medium of English phonology. His grammar/lexis are purely French—but his phonology is English. We normally attribute a certain primacy to grammar/lexis, since in this case we should say 'He's speaking French with an English accent' but not 'He's speaking English, but with French grammar and lexis'.

1.64   Graphology, too, is in a sense *detachable* from the particular language of which it is characteristic. The air traveller in India, for example, notices on one side of his plane, the legend:

INDIAN AIRLINES

इंडियन   एयरलाइन्स

This Devanagari inscription, which might be transliterated īdiyən eyərlains is exponent of a piece of *English* grammar and lexis. It is English expounded in Devanagari (Hindi) graphology.
1.65   It is the detachability of the medium levels from the grammatical/lexical levels which makes phonological and graphological translation possible.
1.7   We have already drawn upon English for examples in this chapter, and we will continue to do so throughout this book. It seems desirable, therefore, to give here the barest outline of the description of English phonology and grammar which we are using. This is not the place to give a full description, even in summary form, of English—but the indications given here will serve to codify what has already been referred to, and will help to elucidate most of the references to English given later.
1.71   *English Phonology.* In English phonology we have a hierarchy of units at four ranks:
(i) *Tone-group*
(ii) *Foot* (or *rhythmic group*)
(iii) *Syllable*
(iv) *Phoneme*

The relation between these is the normal one: i.e. every Tone-group consists of one or more Foot, every Foot of one or more Syllable, every Syllable of one or more Phoneme. Thus || Yes || (with, say, falling tone) is a tone-group, consisting of one foot, consisting of one syllable, consisting of three phonemes. And ‖ What did you | do | yesterday ‖ is a Tone group consisting of three feet. The first foot ‖ What did you | and the last foot | yesterday ‖ each consist of three syllables: the middle foot consists of only one. And the syllables consist of varying numbers of phonemes.

1.711   The *tone-group*. The elements of tone-group structure are T (tonic) which is always present, and P (pretonic) which may be absent. The exponent of T is a *foot*, or more than one foot, which carries one of a system of five contrastive *tones*: the distinctive tone starts on the first syllable (of the first foot) of the tonic. The exponent of P, if present, is one or more foot preceding the tonic, and carrying one of a restricted range of pretonic intonation contours. In these examples tone-group boundaries are marked by ‖ , foot-boundaries by | , the initial syllable of the *tonic* by underlining.

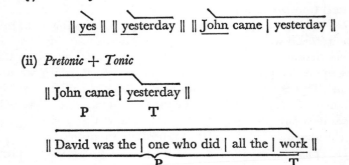

(i) *Tonic only*

‖ yes ‖ ‖ yesterday ‖ ‖ John came | yesterday ‖

(ii) *Pretonic + Tonic*

‖ John came | yesterday ‖
    P   T

‖ David was the | one who did | all the | work ‖
           P   T

1.712   The location of the tonic is significant. It can be shifted from one foot to another, and such shifts are changes of *tonicity*. For example:

‖ David was the | one who did | all the | work ‖
‖ David was the | one who did | all the | work ‖
‖ David was the | one who did | all the | work ‖

14

1.713   The *tone-group*, then, is the unit which carries contrastive *intonation* patterns. The contrasts are of two kinds (i) contrasts of *tone*, i.e. selection of one or another out of a system of five tones operating at the *tonic*: e.g.

1. ‖ y̱ẹs̱ ‖   ＼ falling
2. ‖ y̱ẹs̱ ‖   ／ rising
3. ‖ y̱ẹs̱ ‖   ＿／ low-level + rise
4. ‖ y̱ẹs̱ ‖   ＼／ fall-rise
5. ‖ y̱ẹs̱ ‖   ∧ rise-fall

and (ii) contrasts of *tonicity*, i.e. selection of one or another location for the tonic.

1.714   The *foot*. This is the unit of stress or rhythm. The foot is the carrier of contrastive differences in stress-distribution. The distinctive phonic features of the foot are (i) each foot is expounded, or manifested, by a major chest pulse starting strongly stressed, then falling off (stress-curve ╱‾‾‾＿): if the foot consists of more than one syllable, this means that the first syllable is more strongly stressed than its successor(s), (ii) each foot within one and the same tone-group tends to have approximately the same duration.

The alphabet, for instance, may be recited with various types of foot-division, e.g.

(i)   ‖ A | B | C | D | E̱ ‖
(ii)   ‖ A B | C D | E F̱ | G ‖
(iii)   ‖ A B C | D | E F | G̱ ‖   etc.[5]

1.715   The elements of foot-structure are I (initial, or *ictus*) and R (reduced, or *remiss*)[6]. The exponent of I is always a single syllable. The exponent of R, if present, is one, or more than one,

---

[5] The *feet* and foot-divisions will be most apparent if the reader 'beats time' while reading these aloud, letting the down-beat coincide with the start of each foot.

[6] The terms *ictus* and *remiss* have recently been revived by D. Abercrombie— the first being a traditional term, the second used by Joshua Steele in *Prosodia Rationalis* (1779). They are used by M. A. K. Halliday in his 'The Tones of English', *Archivum Linguisticum*, Vol. XV, Fasc. 1, pp. 1–28, 1964.

syllable. Thus, in the examples above, the feet represented in
‖ A | B | C | . . . etc. each have the structure I. Those repre-
sented by ‖ A B | C D | . . . etc. have the structure IR with a
single syllable as exponent of R, while that represented by
‖ A B C | has the same structure IR, but here R is expounded
by two syllables.

In some cases, the exponent of either I or R is a 'zero syllable'
—that is, a momentary silence, or *rest*, represented by a caret (ᴧ).
The time taken up by the *rest* is usually about that which is
needed to make up the duration of a full foot. When an utterance
begins with an unstressed syllable, we take this to be the exponent
of R in an initial foot, the exponent of I in this case being *rest*.
This appears to be justified by the fact that when such 'incomplete' feet occur immediately after a preceding utterance by the
same speaker there is commonly a momentary silence, which
makes up the time-lapse appropriate to a foot. Thus

$$\| \; _\wedge \; I \mid didn't \mid \underline{go} \; there \; \|$$

1.716   Differences of foot-division are meaningful, being often
the exponents of differences in the structure of grammatical
units: e.g.

1.   ‖ John was a | <u>light</u> house | keeper ‖
2.   ‖ John was a light | <u>house</u> keeper ‖

Here the foot-division before 'light' in 1. marks *light house* as a
compound noun operating as exponent of H in the Ngp. The
foot-division between *light* and *house* in 2. is exponent of a
grammatical division, marking *light* as M in the Ngp, where
house is H.

1.717   The *syllable*. The *syllable* is the unit of syllabicity. Syllables sometimes coincide with feet. When syllable-divisions occur
within a foot their phonic exponent is a momentary retardation
of the major chest-pulse movement.

The elements of syllable-structure are N (nucleus) and K
(consonantal, or marginal element): the latter may be subdivided
as K^r (consonantal syllable-releasing element), K^a (consonantal

syllable-arresting element) and K^i (consonantal inter-nuclear unit[7]). The unit K^i occurs only between two Ns, and cannot be assigned to either of them.

Syllable structures are thus: N, K^rN, NK^a, K^rNK^a, $NK^i(N)$, $(N)K^iN$. Examples: N oh! K^rN tea, spar, straw, NK^a at, and, asks. K^rNK^a top, stop, stops, etc.

The exponents of N are V (simple vowel) or V^v (complex vowel), the exponents of K^r are C (one consonant) or CC or CCC; the exponents of K^a are C, CC, CCC, CCCC.

1.718   The *phoneme*. Phonemes are the units of articulation which operate as exponents of elements of syllable structure. The primary classes are:

V, *vowels*—operating as exponent of N in syllable structure:

   i e a o u ə

^{v}, *glides*—operating alone, or in complex vowels (V^v), as exponent of N: i ə u

C, *consonants:* p b t d k g f v θ ð s z ʃ ʒ h m n ŋ l r w y

1.72   In English *grammar* we recognize a hierarchy of five units:

1. *Sentence*
2. *Clause*
3. *Group*
4. *Word*
5. *Morpheme*

1.721   *Sentence:* The primary elements of sentence-structure are α and β. Sentence-structures which occur are α, β, αβ, βα . . . etc.

Examples: α John arrived yesterday.
            β When John arrived!
            αβ John arrived after we had left.
            βα After we had left, John arrived.   etc.

The exponents of elements of sentence-structure are clauses.

1.722   *Clause.* The primary classes of clause are *free* (operating as exponent of α in sentence-structure) and *bound* (operating as exponent of β in sentence-structure).

---

[7] The *interlude* of C. F. Hockett *Manual of Phonology*, p. 52.

The primary elements of clause structure: S, P, C, A, have been given above (1.33). Primary clause structures include:

SP   e.g. *he/came   they/had arrived*   etc.

$\widehat{SP}$ (S inserted in P)   e.g. *did he come?   had they arrived?*

P (A etc.)   e.g. Come!   Come here.

The exponents of these elements are: P—one, or more than one, Verbal Group (if more than one, the first is finite or non-finite, the other(s) are non-finite), S and C—one, or more than one, Nominal Group, A—one or more than one Adverbial Group.

1.723   *Group.* The primary group classes are *Verbal*, operating at P in clause structure, *Nominal*, operating at S or C in clause structure, and *Adverbial*, operating at A in clause structure.

Since practically no reference is made in the rest of this book to the structure of groups other than Nominal, we confine ourselves here to Nominal Groups.

We have already given the primary elements of Nominal Group structure in 1.43 above: M, H and Q. The structures which actually occur are:

H e.g. John, he, wine, etc.

M . . . H e.g. Old John, red wine, these three old books, etc.

HQ e.g. John the Baptist, people who live in glass houses, etc.

M . . . HQ e.g. the man in the moon, the old man who lives next door, etc.

Secondary elements of Ngp structure, at M are d, o, and e (already exemplified in 1.43 above).

The normal exponents of elements of group structure are *words*. In Ngps, however, we may have *rank-shifted clauses* and *rank-shifted groups* as exponents, e.g. In *What you say is wrong*, *what you say* is a rank-shifted clause (of structure CSP) operating as exponent of H in the Ngp. *What you say.* In the Ngp *the man who came to dinner . . .*, which has the structure MHQ, the exponent of Q is the rank-shifted clause *who came to dinner*. In the Ngp *the man in the moon*, which has the structure MHQ, the exponent of Q is the rank-shifted Adverbial group *in the moon*.

1.724   *Words.* These fall into a large number of classes in terms of their operation in the structure of groups. The primary elements of word-structure are B (base) and A (affix). The exponents of these are morphemes.

1.725   *Morphemes*. These are the smallest meaningful units of grammar. They fall into two primary classes in terms of their operation in the structure of words—*base morphemes*, and *affix morphemes*. Since morphemes are at the 'bottom' of the rank scale they themselves have no structure. In phonological and graphological exponence affix morphemes may be expounded linearly (e.g. the Nominal plural morpheme expounded, most frequently, by a suffixed graphological -s, or phonological / -s, -z, -ᶦz/), or exponentially fused with base morphemes (e.g. *saw* = fused exponence of base morpheme SEE + affix morpheme 'preterite').

1.8   To conclude this introductory chapter we summarize the field of linguistics and the linguistic sciences.

General Linguistics is the general theory of how language works. It provides categories which are applicable in all branches of linguistic science.

General Phonetics is the theory of phonic substance: it provides categories which can be used in the description of the distinctive phonic features of the phonological units of particular languages.

Descriptive Linguistics is the application and extension of general linguistic categories in the description of particular languages.

Comparative Linguistics is an extension of descriptive linguistics which establishes relations between two or more languages. When the languages are separated in space, but not time, it is Synchronic Comparative Linguistics. When they are separated in time, it is Diachronic Comparative Linguistics.

Other parts of the general field of linguistics include Institutional Linguistics and the theory of *Language Varieties* (dealt with in Chapter 13).

Applied Linguistics is a term used to cover all those applications of the theory and categories of general linguistics which go beyond (i) the elucidation of how languages work and (ii) the description of a particular language or languages for its/their own sake. The theory of translation is essentially a theory of applied linguistics.

2

Translation: Definition and General Types

2.0   The theory of translation is concerned with a certain type of relation between languages and is consequently a branch of Comparative Linguistics. From the point of view of translation theory the distinction between synchronic and diachronic comparison is irrelevant. Translation equivalences may be set up, and translations performed, between any pair of languages or dialects—'related' or 'unrelated' and with any kind of spatial, temporal, social or other relationship between them.

Relations between languages can generally be regarded as two-directional, though not always symmetrical. Translation, as a process, is always uni-directional: it is always performed in a given direction. 'from' a *Source Language* 'into' a *Target Language*. Throughout this paper we make use of the abbreviations: SL = Source Language, TL = Target Language.

2.1   *Translation* may be defined as follows:

   the replacement of textual material in one language (SL) by equivalent textual material in another language (TL).

This definition is intentionally wide—not vague, though it may appear so at first sight. Two lexical items in it call for comment. These are 'textual material' (where 'text' might have been expected) and 'equivalent'.

The use of the term 'textual material' underlines the fact that in normal conditions it is not the entirety of a SL text which is translated, that is, replaced by TL *equivalents*. At one or more levels of language there may be simple replacement, by non-equivalent TL material: for example, if we translate the English text *What time is it?* into French as *Quelle heure est-il?* there is replacement of SL (English) grammar and lexis by *equivalent* TL (French) grammar and lexis. There is also *replacement* of SL graphology by TL graphology—but the TL graphological form is by no means a translation *equivalent* of the SL graphological form.

Moreover, at one or more levels there may be no replacement at all, but simple transference of SL material into the TL text. On this, see Chapter 6 below.

The term 'equivalent' is clearly a key term, and as such is discussed at length below. The central problem of translation-practice is that of finding TL translation equivalents. A central task of translation theory is that of defining the nature and conditions of translation equivalence.

Before going on to discuss the nature of translation equivalence it will be useful to define some broad types or categories of translation in terms of the *extent* (2.2), *levels* (2.3), and *ranks* (2.4) of translation.

2.2   *Full vs. Partial* translation. This distinction relates to the *extent* (in a syntagmatic sense) of SL text which is submitted to the translation process. By *text* we mean any stretch of language, spoken or written, which is under discussion. According to cir-cumstances a text may thus be a whole library of books, a single volume, a chapter, a paragraph, a sentence, a clause . . . etc. It may also be a fragment not co-extensive with any formal literary or linguistic unit.

2.21   In a *full* translation the entire text is submitted to the translation process: that is, every part of the SL text is replaced by TL text material.

2.22   In a *partial* translation, some part or parts of the SL text are left untranslated: they are simply transferred to and incor-porated in the TL text. In literary translation it is not uncommon for some SL lexical items to be treated in this way, either because they are regarded as 'untranslatable' or for the deliberate purpose of introducing 'local colour' into the TL text. This process of transferring SL lexical items into a TL text is more complex than appears at first sight, and it is only approximately true to say that they remain 'untranslated': on this, see 6.31.

2.23   The distinction between full and partial translation is hardly a (linguistically) technical one. It is dealt with here, however, since it is important to use the distinct term *partial* in this semi-technical, syntagmatic, sense, reserving the term *restricted* for use in the linguistically technical sense given in 2.3.

2.3   *Total vs. Restricted* translation. This distinction relates to the *levels* of language involved in translation.

2.31   By *total* translation we mean what is most usually meant by 'translation'; that is, translation in which all levels of the SL text are replaced by TL material. Strictly speaking, 'total' translation is a misleading term, since, though total *replacement* is involved it is not replacement by *equivalents* at all levels (cf. 2.1 above).

In 'total' translation SL grammar and lexis are replaced by equivalent TL grammar and lexis. This replacement entails the replacement of SL phonology/graphology by TL phonology/graphology, but this is not normally replacement by TL *equivalents*, hence there is no translation, in our sense, at that level[1]. For use as a technical term, *Total Translation* may best be defined as:

replacement of SL grammar and lexis by equivalent TL grammar and lexis with consequential replacement of SL phonology/graphology by (non-equivalent) TL phonology/graphology.

2.32   By *restricted translation* we mean:

replacement of SL textual material by equivalent TL textual material, at only one level,

that is translation performed only at the phonological or at the graphological level, or at only one of the two levels of grammar and lexis.

It should be noted that, though phonological or graphological translation is possible, there can be no analogous 'contextual translation'—that is translation restricted to the inter-level of context but not entailing translation at the grammatical or lexical levels. In other words there is no way in which we can replace SL 'contextual units' by equivalent TL 'contextual units' without *simultaneously* replacing SL grammatical/lexical units by equivalent TL grammatical/lexical units, since it is only by virtue

[1] Occasionally there is concomitant replacement by a TL form which is phonologically equivalent, or nearly equivalent, to the SL form at the phonological level, as when Jap. *iie* is translated by (Amer.) Eng. *yeah*, as it may be in certain cases (see 5.6). When this happens in total translation it is normally purely accidental. Rare cases of deliberate attempts at partial replacement by *equivalent* TL phonology, in total translation, do occur: e.g. in film 'dubbing' and translation of poetry.

of their encapsulation, so to say, in formal linguistic units that 'contextual units' exist. Context is, in fact, the organization of situation-substance into units which are co-extensive with and operationally inseparable from the formal units of grammar and lexis. With the medium levels the situation is different. Phonology, for instance, is the organization of phonic substance into units which, in combination, function as exponents of the units of grammar and lexis; phonological units, as such, are not bound to grammatical or lexical units in the way in which contextual units are bound to such units. Hence the separability of phonology/graphology for translation purposes; and, on the other hand, the non-separability of context.

2.321   In *phonological* translation SL phonology is replaced by equivalent TL phonology, but there are no other replacements except such grammatical or lexical changes as may result accidentally from phonological translation: e.g. an English plural, such as *cats*, may come out as apparently a singular *cat* in phonological translation into a language which has no final consonant clusters.

2.322   In *graphological* translation SL graphology is replaced by equivalent TL graphology, with no other replacements, except, again, accidental changes.

2.323   Phonological translation is practised deliberately by actors and mimics who assume foreign or regional 'accents'— though seldom in a self-conscious or fully consistent way (i.e. except in the case of particularly good mimics, the phonological translation is usually only partial). The phonetic/phonological performance of foreign-language learners is another example of (involuntary and often partial) phonological translation. Graphological translation is sometimes practised deliberately, for special typographic effects, and also occurs involuntarily in the performance of persons writing a foreign language.

Both phonological and graphological translation must be included in a general theory of translation because they help to throw light on the conditions of translation equivalence, and hence on the more complex process of total translation.

2.324   Graphological translation must not be confused with *transliteration*. The latter is a complex process involving phonological translation with the addition of phonology-graphology correlation at both ends of the process, i.e. in SL and TL. In transliteration, SL graphological units are first replaced by corresponding SL phonological units; these SL phonological units are translated into equivalent TL phonological units; finally the TL phonological units are replaced by corresponding TL graphological units. But the process is further complicated in ways discussed in Chapter 10 below.

2.325   Restricted translation at the *grammatical* and *lexical* levels means, respectively, replacement of SL grammar by equivalent TL grammar, but with no replacement of lexis, and replacement of SL lexis by equivalent TL lexis but with no replacement of grammar. 'Pure' translation restricted to either of these levels is difficult if not impossible owing to the close interrelations between grammar and lexis and the tendency for exponents of grammatical categories to be 'fused' with exponents of lexical items. Since the grammatical categories of a language are relatively high-level abstractions, 'pure' statements of grammatical equivalences can best be presented as formulaic equations: but this is not translation, which is an operation performed on a specific SL *text*. Grammatical *translation* requires that the SL text be replaced by a text which is purely TL in its grammar, but still retains all the SL lexical items. On this, see below.

2.4   *Rank of Translation.* A third type of differentiation in translation relates to the *rank* in a grammatical (or phonological) hierarchy at which translation equivalence is established.

In normal total translation the grammatical units between which translation equivalences are set up may be at any rank, and in a long text the ranks at which translation equivalence occur are constantly changing: at one point, the equivalence is sentence-to-sentence, at another, group-to-group, at another word-to-word, etc., not to mention formally 'shifted' or 'skewed' equivalences (see Chapter 12).

It is possible, however, to make a translation which is *total* in the sense given in 2.31 above, but in which the selection of TL equivalents is deliberately confined to *one rank* (or a few ranks, low in the rank scale) in the hierarchy of grammatical units. We may call this *rank-bound* translation. The cruder attempts at Machine

Translation are rank-bound in this sense, usually at word or morpheme rank; that is, they set up word-to-word or morpheme-to-morpheme equivalences, but not equivalences between high-rank units such as the group, clause or sentence. In contrast with this, normal total translation in which equivalences shift freely up and down the rank scale may be termed *unbounded* translation.

2.41 In rank-bound translation, as we have said, an attempt is made always to select TL equivalents at the same rank, e.g. word. A word-rank-bound translation is useful for certain purposes, for instance, for illustrating in a crude way differences between the SL and the TL in the structure of higher-rank units —as in some kinds of interlinear translation of texts in 'exotic' languages. Often, however, rank-bound translation is 'bad' translation, in that it involves using TL equivalents which are not appropriate to their location in the TL text, and which are not justified by the interchangeability of SL and TL texts in one and the same situation (see Chapter 7).

2.42 The popular terms *free*, *literal*, and *word-for-word* translation, though loosely used, partly correlate with the distinctions dealt with here. A *free* translation is always *unbounded*—equivalences shunt up and down the rank scale, but tend to be at the higher ranks—sometimes between larger units than the sentence. *Word-for-word* translation generally means what its says: i.e. is essentially *rank-bound* at word-rank (but may include some morpheme-morpheme equivalences). *Literal* translation lies between these extremes; it may start, as it were, from a word-for-word translation, but make changes in comformity with TL grammar (e.g. inserting additional words, changing structures at any rank, etc.); this may make it a group-group or clause-clause translation. One notable point, however, is that literal translation, like word-for-word, tends to remain *lexically* word-for-word, i.e. to use the highest (unconditioned) probability lexical equivalent for each lexical item.[2] *Lexical* adaptation to TL collocational or 'idiomatic' requirements seems to be characteristic of *free* translation, as in this example:

UNIVERSITY OF WINDSOR LIBRARY

SL text   It's raining cats and dogs.

[2] On equivalance-probabilities, see 3.3 below.

141461

TL text 1	Il est pleuvant chats et chiens.	(Word-for-word)
2	Il pleut des chats et des chiens.	(Literal)
3	Il pleut à verse.	(Free)

Here 1 is *word-word*, 2 is *group-group* (with TL structural 'normalizations' within two of the groups). 3, since it changes the clause-structure from SPC to SPA, must, perhaps, be regarded as clause-clause: it also introduces a TL lexical normalization. Only 3, the free translation, is interchangeable with the SL text in situations.

Another example of *free* translation (switching to full sentence-equivalence) would be this Russian–English one:

SL text	Bog s n'im'i!	
TL text 1	God with them!	(Word-for-word)
2	God is with them!	(Literal)
3	Never mind about them!	(Free)

Once again, only 3, the free translation, is interchangeable with the SL text in a situation where the addressee is being advised to dismiss or disregard a triviality.

3

Translation Equivalence

WE have to distinguish between, on the one hand, translation equivalence as an empirical phenomenon, discovered by comparing SL and TL texts; and, on the other hand, the underlying conditions, or justification, of translation equivalence. The conditions of translation equivalence are discussed in Chapter 7. Here we are concerned only with translation equivalence as an empirical phenomenon.

3.1 A further distinction must be made between *textual equivalence* and *formal correspondence*. A textual equivalent is any TL text or portion of text which is observed on a particular occasion, by methods described below, to be the equivalent of a given SL text or portion of text. A formal correspondent, on the other hand, is any TL category (unit, class, structure, element of structure, etc.) which can be said to occupy, as nearly as possible, the 'same' place in the 'economy' of the TL as the given SL category occupies in the SL. Since every language is ultimately *sui generis*—its categories being defined in terms of relations holding within the language itself—it is clear that formal correspondence is nearly always approximate.

3.2 A *textual translation equivalent*, then, is any TL form (text or portion of text) which is observed to be the equivalent of a given SL form (text or portion of text).

3.21 The discovery of textual equivalents is based on the authority of a competent bilingual informant or translator. Thus, to find the French textual equivalent of the English text *My son is six*, we ask a competent translator to put this into the TL, French. He supplies *Mon fils a six ans*[1]. This, then, is the textual equivalent of *My son is six*. We may repeat this process for any portion of the full text—asking, for instance, for the French equivalent of

---

[1] It should be noted that this, and almost all other examples in this paper, are decontextualized texts: consequently the equivalents given are merely *probable* (in this case highly probable). Some of them might be different in special contexts.

My son in this text. The translator supplies the equivalent *Mon fils*.

3.22   In place of *asking* for equivalents we may adopt a more formal procedure, namely, *commutation* and observation of concomitant variation. In other words we may systematically introduce changes into the SL text and observe what changes if any occur in the TL text as a consequence. A *textual translation equivalent* is thus: *that portion of a TL text which is changed when and only when a given portion of the SL text is changed*. In our present example, having had *My son is six* translated into French we might ask for the translation of *Your daughter is six*. The TL text this time is *Votre fille a six ans*. The changed portion of the TL text (Mon fils/Votre fille) is then taken to be the equivalent of the changed portion of the SL text (My son/Your daughter).

3.221   In simple cases like the above, one generally relies on one's own knowledge of the languages involved. This is the only thing one can do with a recorded (spoken or written) text when the original translator is not present. In such a case, the investigator acts as his own informant and discovers textual equivalents 'intuitively'—i.e. by drawing on his own experience, without necessarily going through an overt procedure of commutation. Nevertheless, commutation is the ultimate test for textual equivalence, and it is useful in cases where equivalence is not of the simple equal-rank and unit-to-unit type illustrated above.

3.222   For example, given the English SL text The woman came out of the house, and its Russian TL equivalent Ženščina vyšla iz domu, we might wish to discover the Russian equivalent of the English *definite article* in the group The woman in this text. Commutation might give the following result:

> SL text 1   The woman came out of the house.
> TL text 1   Ženščina vyšla iz domu.
> SL text 2   A woman came out of the house.
> TL text 2   Iz domu vyšla ženščina.

We would thus establish that, in this particular position in this particular text, the change of English *the* to *a* is correlated with a change in the *sequence of elements* in the structure of the Russian *clause*. We can state this textual equivalence as:

$$\text{Eng. } the \text{ in (N) at } /S/ = \text{Rus. } /\overrightarrow{SPA}/$$

$$\text{Eng. } a \text{ in (N) at } /S/ = \text{Rus. } /\overleftarrow{SPA}/$$

This may be read as 'English *the*, a term in a system operating in a Nominal Group, at the place in Clause-structure, Subject, has as its Russian translation equivalent the indicated sequence (Subject, Predicator, Adjunct) of elements in the Russian clause structure', and, further, 'English *a*, a term . . . etc., has its translation equivalent, the *inverse* sequence of elements in the Russian clause'.

3.223   In some cases there is *no* TL equivalent of a given SL item, and commutation may again be used to demonstrate this. It is useful to say in such cases that the TL equivalent is *nil*, reserving the term *zero* for use, if at all, when zero is a term operating in a TL system. Thus, to take another example, comparing the following English SL text and TL texts in French and Russian, we see a possible use for the distinction between *zero* and *nil*.

SL Eng.   My father was a doctor.
TL Fr.   Mon père était docteur.
TL Rus.   Otets u men'a byl doktor.

One might describe the system of *articles* in both French and English as containing a term *zero*. In the present example, then, we could say that the translation equivalent of the English indefinite article, *a*, is the French article *zero*. Russian, however, has no system of articles. In the Russian text, therefore, there is no translation equivalent of the English indefinite article. We say, then, that the Russian equivalent of *a* in this text is *nil*. Equivalence, in this example, can be established only at a higher rank, namely the *group*. The English nominal group *a doctor* has as its equivalent the Russian nominal group *doktor*. In general, *nil* equivalence at one rank implies that equivalence can only be established at a higher rank.

3.3   In a text of any length, some specific SL items are almost certain to occur several times. At each occurrence there will be a specific TL textual equivalent. Having observed each *particular* textual equivalent, we can then make a *general* statement of textual equivalences for each SL item, covering all its occurrences in the text as a whole. At each occurrence, the particular SL item may always have the same TL equivalent. The statement of general textual equivalence in this case is qualitatively the same as that of particular textual equivalence; but there is a difference, namely that it can be *quantified*. We may express it in the actual figures, e.g. 'SL item X occurs 79 times in this text, and its TL equivalent is x in every case'; or as a percentage, 'SL X = TL x, 100%'; or, finally, as a *probability*, in terms of the probability scale in which 1 means 'absolute certainty' and 0 means 'absolute impossibility', 'SL X = TL x, 1', i.e. 'SL X has, as its textual equivalent, TL x, with the probability 1'. This means that if you choose any occurrence of X in the SL text at random, it is certain that its TL equivalent will be x.

3.31   Frequently occurring SL items commonly have more than one TL equivalent in the course of a long text. Each particular equivalent occurs a specific number of times: by dividing the number of occurrences of each particular equivalent by the total number of occurrences of the SL item we obtain the equivalence-probability of each particular equivalence. For example, in a French short story of about 12,000 words the preposition *dans* occurs 134 times. The textual equivalent of this in an English translation is *in* in 98 occurrences, *into* in 26, *from* in 2, and *about* and *inside* in one occurrence each; there are six occurrences of *dans* where the equivalent is either nil, or not an English pre-position. (The short study from which these figures are taken did not further differentiate these six cases.) In terms of probabilities we can state the translation equivalences as follows: *dans = in* ·73, *dans = into* ·19, *dans = from* ·015, *dans = about/inside* ·0075. This means that if you select any occurrence of *dans* at random in this text, the probability that its translation equivalent on that occasion is *in* is ·73, the probability that it is *into* is ·19, etc.

3.32   The probability values given so far are based on the assumption that, at each occurrence, the probability of a particular equivalence is the same as it is at every other occurrence; that is to say, they are *unconditioned probabilities*. But the equivalence-probabilities are, in fact, constantly affected by contextual and *co-textual* factors[2]. We must, then, take these factors into account, and consider not merely the unconditioned probabilities, but also the *conditioned probabilities* of the various equivalences. Thus, though the unconditioned probability of the equivalence *dans = into* is only ·19, the conditioned probability of this equivalence is very much higher when *dans* is preceded by certain verbs, e.g. *aller*, and must be 1 (certainty), or very nearly so, when such a 'verb of motion' precedes, and a 'noun referring to a place' follows.

Provided the sample is big enough, translation-equivalence-probabilities may be generalized to form 'translation rules' applicable to other texts, and perhaps to the 'language as a whole' —or, more strictly, to all texts within the same *variety* of the language (the same dialect, register, etc.—see Chapter 13).

3.4   A *translation rule* is thus an extrapolation of the probability values of textual translation equivalences. Such a rule is a statement of highest unconditioned probability equivalence, supplemented by highest conditioned probability equivalences, with an indication of the conditioning factors. For human translators the rules can make appeal to *contextual* meaning (e.g. *'dans*—translate as *in* unless a verb of motion precedes and a place-noun follows' or the like). For the purpose of Machine Translation, translation rules may be operational instructions for *co-textual search* for items marked in the machine glossary by particular diacritics, with instructions to print out the particular conditioned equivalent in each case. Such operational instructions, which if followed, can be guaranteed with a high degree of probability to produce a 'correct' result, are known as *algorithms*. The looser, more contextually based, instructions for human translators are 'translation rules'; the more rigid, co-textually based, instructions for MT are, strictly speaking, 'translation-algorithms'. In general, to be effective, translation algorithms must be based on equivalences with probabilities approaching 1.

[2] By *context* we mean 'context of situation', i.e. those elements of the extra-textual situation which are related to the text as being linguistically relevant: hence *contextual*. By *co-text* we mean items in the *text* which accompany the item under discussion: hence *co-textual*.

4

Formal Correspondence

In 3.1 above we alluded to the distinction between textual equivalence and formal correspondence. A formal correspondent is any TL category which may be said to occupy, as nearly as possible, the 'same' place in the economy of the TL as the given SL category occupies in the SL.

4.1   It is clear that formal correspondence can be only approxmate, and that it can be most easily established at relatively high levels of abstraction. Thus, if we find that two languages operate each with grammatical units at five ranks (an example might be English and French, both of which appear to have five ranks: sentence, clause, group, word, morpheme) we can reasonably say that there is formal correspondence between the two hierarchies of units; each has the same number of ranks, and as (taxonomic) hierarchies each has the same kind of relationship between units of the different ranks. Having established such a highly abstract correspondence, we may use this as a frame of reference for stating approximate correspondence at lower abstractional levels; e.g. we may talk of formal correspondence between SL and TL elements of structure operating at 'corresponding' ranks.

4.2   It may be, however, that formal correspondence can only be established ultimately on the basis of textual equivalence at some point. Thus we may state that an item or class of one language is the formal equivalent of an item or class in another, because the category in question operates in approximately the same way in the structure of higher rank units in both languages; but this in turn, implies that we have established a correspondence between these higher rank units, and this may have to be done on the basis of highest probability textual equivalence.

4.21   For example, we might say that there is formal correspondence between the word-classes *preposition* in English and French. This statement is based on the fact that in both languages the word-class labelled 'preposition' functions along with nominal groups in the structure of adverbial phrases, which in turn function in both languages as (i) *qualifiers* in nominal group structure (e.g. the door *of the house*—la porte *de la maison*) or (ii) as *adjuncts* in clause structure. But this clearly pushes the problem of justifying our statement of formal correspondence further up the rank scale; we still have to justify the correspondence of nominal groups, adjuncts, etc., and this might have to be done on the basis of textual equivalence.

4.3 In spite of its approximate nature, and the theoretical difficulty of its justification, the concept of 'formal correspondence' is a useful one; indeed, it is an essential basis for the discussion of problems which are important to translation theory and necessary for its application (see Chapter 12).

4.31 Formal correspondence is of interest from another point of view as well; namely that the degree of divergence between textual equivalence and formal correspondence may perhaps be used as a measure of typological difference between languages. This can be exemplified by considering formal correspondence and textual equivalence between English prepositions and certain formal classes in French and Kabardian (a N.W. Caucasian language).

4.311 In the French text referred to above there are 1220 occurrences of prepositions. In the English TL text 910 of these have a preposition as textual translation equivalent: for this text, the unconditioned equivalence-probability of the equivalence *Fr. preposition = Eng. preposition* is ·75. We are justified in saying that for English and French prepositions there is a fairly high degree of convergence between formal correspondence and textual equivalence; and this may be taken as a symptom of typological similarity.

4.312 The establishment of formal correspondences between English and Kabardian is more difficult; for one thing, it is probable that Kabardian has only four ranks of grammatical units as compared with the five of English. We may, however, roughly equate units of the lowest rank in both languages, labelling both *morphemes*. In Kabardian there is a class of bound morphemes which may be called 'relational preverbs'. These are prefixed to verbal morphemes, forming together with them (and certain other morphemes) verbal units which function as predicators in clause structure. Formally, it is reasonable to say that these relational preverbs correspond most closely to English bound morphemes such as *in- ex-* etc., which occur prefixed to verbs; in other words, Kabardian relational preverbs are *formal correspondents* of English verbal prefixes. No actual figures for textual equivalence are available, but it is almost certain that the highest-probability English *textual equivalents* of Kabardian relational preverbs are prepositions. There is thus considerable divergence between formal correspondence and textual equivalence as between English prepositions and Kabardian relational preverbs. This is what one might expect in the case of a pair of languages which are both typologically and genetically very different; more precisely, the divergence shown here may be taken to be a symptom of typological difference, which parallels genetic unrelatedness.

5

Meaning and Total Translation

IT is generally agreed that *meaning* is important in translation—
particularly in total translation. Indeed, translation has often
been defined with reference to meaning; a translation is said to
'have the same meaning' as the original. Dostert defines translation as 'that branch of the applied science of language which is
specifically concerned with the problem—or the fact—of the
transference of meaning from one set of patterned symbols . . .
into another set of patterned symbols . . .'[1]

It is clearly necessary for translation-theory to draw upon a
theory of meaning; without such a theory certain important
aspects of the translation process cannot be discussed, nor can
statements like that of Dostert be evaluated. In terms of the
theory of meaning which we make use of here—a theory deriving
largely from the views of J. R. Firth—the view that SL and TL
texts 'have the same meaning' or that 'transference of meaning'
occurs in translation is untenable.

5.1   Meaning, in our view, is a property of a language. An SL
text has an SL meaning, and a TL text has a TL meaning—a
Russian text, for instance, has a Russian meaning (as well as
Russian phonology/graphology, grammar and lexis), and an
equivalent English text has an English meaning. This is necessarily the case, since, following Firth, we define *meaning* as the
total network of relations entered into by any linguistic form—
text, item-in-text, structure, element of structure, class, term in
system—or whatever it may be.

The relations entered into by the formal linguistic units of
grammar and lexis are of two kinds (i) *formal* relations, (ii)
contextual relations.

5.11   By *formal relations* we mean relations between one formal
item and others in the same language. In *grammar* this may be the
relation between units of different rank in the grammatical hier-

[1] Locke and Booth *Machine Translation of Languages* (New York, London
1955), p. 124.

archy, the relation between terms in a system, the relation between a class and an element of structure at a higher rank, co-textual relations between grammatical classes or items in a text, and so on. In *lexis* there are formal relations between one lexical item and others in the same lexical set, and formal co-textual (collocational) relations between lexical items in texts.

The various formal relations into which a form enters constitute its *formal meaning*.

5.12   By *contextual relations* we mean the relationship of grammatical or lexical items to linguistically relevant elements in the situations in which the items operate as, or in, texts. Those situational elements which are contextually 'relevant' to a given grammatical or lexical item are discovered, just as translation equivalents are discovered, by commutation. Change an element in the situation and observe what textual change occurs; change an item in a text and observe what situational changes occur. The *range* of situational elements which are thus found to be relevant to a given linguistic form constitute the *contextual meaning* of that form.

5.2   Now since every language is formally *sui generis* and formal correspondence is, at best, a rough approximation, it is clear that the *formal* meanings of SL items and TL items can rarely be the same. A TL *dual* may on occasion be the translation equivalent of an SL *plural*—for instance, Arabic **kitaabeen** as equivalent of English *books*—but it cannot have the same *formal* meaning. One is a term in a 2-term number-system, the other a term in a 3-term system; each gets a 'value'[2] deriving from the co-existence of the other term(s) in the system. We cannot, therefore, talk about formal meaning being 'transferred' from SL to TL.

The same is true of contextual meanings. The contextual meaning of an item is the groupment of relevant situational features with which it is related. This groupment varies from one language to another. It is rarely the same in any two languages, and it is, moreover, related to formal meaning; thus, if we have two systems containing different numbers of terms (and hence differing as to the formal meanings of these terms) we will find that

---

[2] In the Saussurean sense: this formal 'value' of terms in a formal system is also what is quantified as 'information' in information theory.

at least some of the terms also have different contextual meanings.
5.3   Consider, for instance, two different systems of deictics or
demonstratives: one, a three-term system found in N.E. Scots
dialects (this–that–yon), the other, the four-term system of
Standard English (this–these–that–those). If we assume that both
systems cover approximately the same total contextual field we
can represent the contextual meanings of the constituent terms
diagrammatically as follows:

	S	P
I	this	these
II	that	those

St. E.

this	1
that	2
yon	3

N.E. Sco.

The Standard English system is represented here as contextually 2-dimensional: it embodies two degrees of deixis (I, II)
and two numbers (Singular, Plural). The N.E. Scots system is
unidimensional, embodying only deixis—3 degrees this time
(1, 2, 3). Numerosity is a contextually irrelevant feature of
situations for the N.E. Scots system.

It is clear that if we translate from Standard English to Scots we
cannot 'transfer meaning'. There is no way in which, for example,
Scots *that* can be said to 'mean the same' as English *that* or *this*
or *these* or *those*. On a given occasion it may refer to, or be relatable to, the same feature of the situation as one of the English
deictics—but its formal and contextual *meaning* is clearly different.
5.4   A more extended example will make this point clearer.
Imagine a situation in which a girl walks in and says 'I've
arrived'. The situation in which this text occurs is, like all
situations, indefinitely complex, in the sense that in an attempt
to describe it exhaustively one could go on sub-describing with
greater and greater delicacy to a degree ultimately limited only
by the refinement of our language of description. We might begin,
for example, by specifying the precise time, date and location, the
girl's name, age, height, weight, colour of eyes and hair, her

clothes, profession, religion, relationships to other people; the number and nature of her audience . . . and so on.

5.41 However, only very few features of the situation are linguistically relevant; that is to say, are built into the contextual meaning of the text and its parts. These include the following:

(i) one participant in the situation, identified only as the *performer* of the linguistic act (in this case, the *speaker*) and correlated with selection of the pronoun *I* as opposed to *we, you, he*, etc., or a noun such as *Mary*.

(ii) an *arrival*—a complex event which need not be further described here, correlated with selection of the lexical item ARRIVE as opposed to, say, LEAVE or EAT, etc.

(iii) a *prior event* which is

(iv) *linked* to a current situation; these two together being correlated with selection of a *perfect* form (*have arrived*) as opposed to a non-perfect (*arrive, arrived*, etc.).

(v) the 'current situation' in this case is *present*, and this correlates with selection of *non-preterite* (*have* arrived) as opposed to preterite (*had* arrived) . . . etc.[3]

5.42 Now suppose the text is translated into Russian as *ja prišla*.

The relevant features of the situation now include:

(i) a *speaker*—selection of *ja* (as opposed to *my, ty*, etc.)

(ii) the speaker is *female*—selection of *prišla* (as opposed to *prišel*)

(iii) an *arrival*—selection of PRIITI (as opposed to VYITI, etc.)

(iv) on *foot*—selection of PRIITI (as opposed to PRIEXAT')

(v) a *prior event*—selection of *past* (as opposed to *present*, etc.)

(vi) *completed* on a specific occasion—selection of *perfective* (determinate) verb-form (as opposed to *imperfective*) . . . etc.

5.43 Clearly, though the Russian text is a perfectly good translation-equivalent of the English text, it does not 'mean the same'—since it selects as linguistically (contextually) relevant a different set of elements in the situation. We can tabulate the difference thus:

[3] This list could be extended to cover the contextual meanings of the *Sentence*, the *Clause-Structure* (SP), of *Nominal Group, Verbal Group*, etc., but the list given here is sufficient for our purpose.

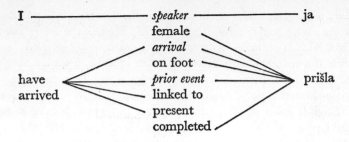

Only the situational features italicized in the list are contextually relevant to both the SL and the TL text.

Such examples could be multiplied indefinitely. We will give only two further illustrations at this point.

5.5   A Burushin[4] is talking about his brother. In the course of the conversation he frequently uses the item *a-cho*. The interpreter translates this *my brother*. The Burushin is now replaced by his sister. She, too, talks about the same person, who is, of course, also *her* brother; she says *a-yas*[5]. The interpreter translates as before: *my brother*.

5.51   Now, an Englishman might say 'The interpreter translated *a-cho* by *my brother*. He is a good interpreter, so we may assume that "my brother" *means the same* as "a-cho" '. But, on the second occasion, the interpreter translates *a-yas* by *my brother*. So the Englishman—still trusting the interpreter—has to admit that *my brother* 'means the same as' *a-yas*. Further pressed, he asserts that *my brother* 'means the same' on both occasions. Now, since the first 'my brother' means the same as the second 'my brother' he must conclude that the two Burushaski items which 'mean the same' as 'my brother' also mean the same as each other.

At this point the Englishman, being an explorer or a travelling salesman, undismayed by the unlikelihood of free variation, refuses to discuss the matter further. The linguist, however, cannot let the matter rest there. Unless *a-cho* and *a-yas* are free variants, then they cannot 'mean the same' as each other. It is

    [4] That is, a speaker of *Burushaski*, the language of the Nagir and Hunza States in the Gilgit Agency, in the extreme N.W. of Pakistan.
    [5] The *a-* in these examples is an (obligatory) pronominal prefix—the lexical items are *cho* and *yas*.

clear, then, that *neither* of them can mean the same as *my brother*; for *my brother*, as the Englishman said, 'means the same' both times. This is certainly true from an English point of view, and this is the only linguistically valid point of view, since *my brother*, being an English item, has an English meaning. It is equally true that *a-cho* and *a-yas*, though they seem to 'mean the same' from an English point of view, do *not* mean the same from a Burushaski point of view; and this, again, is the only linguistically valid point of view, since, being Burushaski items, they have Burushaski meanings.

5.52   In fact, of course, *brother* and *cho* do not 'mean the same'. There is no 'transference of meaning' here; only replacement of Burushaski items by an English translation equivalent. The situational elements which are, so to speak, encapsulated in the contextual meaning of *brother* might be roughly characterized as *male* and *sibling*: those which are encapsulated in the contextual meaning of *cho* are *sibling* and *of same sex as speaker*. The relationship of the English and Burushaski lexical items to elements in the situation can be tabulated as follows: (in this table + means *male*, — means *female*)

English	Situation		Burushaski
	Speaker	Sibling	
brother	+	+	cho
	—	+	yas
sister	+	—	
	—	—	cho

5.6   By a curious coincidence we can diagrammatize the contextual meaning of terms in the (grammatical) closed system of 'acceptance–rejection' items (yes–no) in exactly the same way. In English, selection of *yes* or *no* in response to a question (or statement) depends on what we may call 'the polarity of the situation': situation positive, answer 'yes'; situation negative, answer 'no' (irrespective of the polarity of the preceding utterance). In many other languages (e.g. at least some Slavonic languages, Arabic, Japanese, at least some Bantu languages), selection of the appropriate response depends on the polarity-relationship between question (or statement) and situation: *same polarity*—answer *X*; *different polarity*—answer *Y*. Some languages (e.g. French, with *oui*, *si*, *non*, and Norwegian and Swedish, with *ja*, *jo*, *nej*) have a three-term system here.

We illustrate with English, Japanese and French:

		Question	Situation	Eng.	Jap.	Fr.
e.g. Did you?	I did.	+	+	yes	hai	oui
Didn't you?	I did.	−	+		iie	si
Did you?	I didn't.	+	−	no		non
Didn't you?	I didn't.	−	−		hai	

We cannot say that English *yes* 'means the same' as Japanese *hai* or French *oui*, though in certain situations *hai* and *oui* may be the appropriate translation equivalents of *yes*.

5.7 Another manifestation of the 'same-meaning' or 'meaning-transference' fallacy is seen in the view that translation is a 'transcoding' process, a well-known example being Weaver's remark: 'When I look at an article in Russian, I say: "This is really written in English, but it has been coded in some strange symbols. I will now proceed to decode".'[6]

This implies either that there is a one-to-one relationship between English and Russian grammatical/lexical items and their contextual meanings, or that there is some pre-existent 'message' with an independent meaning of its own which can be presented or expounded now in one 'code' (Russian) now in another 'code' (English). But this is to ignore the fact that each 'code' (i.e. each language) carries with it its own particular meaning, since meaning, as we have said in 5.1 above, is 'a property of a

[6] In Locke and Booth *Machine Translation of Languages* (New York, London 1955), p. 18.

language'. The one thing which does most nearly correspond to transcoding is the universal literate practice of switching from the spoken to the written medium and vice versa. In this process, one and the same 'message' embodied in a particular selection of grammatical and lexical forms may be presented, or expounded, alternatively in two different 'codes'. Thus the 'message' discussed in 5.4 above may be expounded in the written medium as *I've arrived* and in the spoken medium in a phonological form represented here in the transcription ‖ 1. ˌaⁱvə | raⁱvd ‖ . The passage from one to the other of these two exponential forms of the message might legitimately be called 'transcoding'—but this is not translation.

It is possible that the 'transcoding' view is an operationally useful one for machine translation, in its cruder forms at least, where the problem is that of setting up algorithms which will produce moderately intelligible translations with a high degree of probability. But for the deeper understanding of the translation process the 'transcoding' view is not useful.

5.8   Our objection to 'transcoding' or 'transference of meaning' is not a mere terminological quibble. There are two main reasons why translation theory cannot operate with the 'transference of meaning' idea. In the first place, it is a misrepresentation of the process, and consequently renders the discussion of the conditions of translation equivalence difficult; in the second place, it conceals the fact that a useful distinction can be made between *translation* and another process which we call *transference*. In transference, which we discuss in the next section, there is, indeed, transference of meaning; but this is not translation in the usual sense.

6

Transference

IN normal translation, as we have said above, the TL text has
a *TL meaning*. That is to say, the 'values' of TL items are entirely
those set up by formal and contextual relations in the TL itself.
There is no carry-over into the TL of values set up by formal or
contextual relations in the SL.

It is, however, possible to carry out an operation in which the
TL text, or, rather, parts of the TL text, do have *values set up in
the SL*: in other words, have *SL meanings*. We call this process
transference.

6.1   A good example of transference of the formal and contextual meanings of lexical items is found in an article in *Language*
on colour terms in Navaho[1]. We will say more about Navaho
colour terms later (see 7.41 below): meanwhile we consider only
two ɬico and dootl'iž. These terms belong in a lexical set of only
three terms covering approximately the whole spectrum—a situational range covered in English by six terms (red, orange, yellow, green, blue, purple).[2] Consequently, the formal meanings of
the Navaho terms must be different from those of the English
terms. The contextual meanings of the two Navaho terms given
here are also different from anything in English: ɬico means approximately the same as *yellow + orange*, and dootl'iž as *green +
blue + purple*.

6.11   Now, for the purpose of 'translation', the authors of the
article coin two new 'English' colour terms: (it is) *yoo* ('yellow-
or-orange') as the 'translation equivalent' of ɬico, and (it is)
bogop ('blue-or-green-or-purple') as the 'translation equivalent'

[1] Landar, Ervin and Horowitz, 'Navaho Color Categories', *Language*, 36.3(1)
(1960), p. 368. For typographic reasons some slight transcriptional alterations
have been made here.

[2] Or *seven* if we use the time-honoured, but slightly technical, series
ROYGBIV, with *indigo* and *violet*. The whole treatment of colour and colour-
relations is somewhat over-simplified here and in 7.41. This does not, however,
in any way affect the *principle* under discussion.

of dootl'iž. We put the term 'translation equivalent' in quotes, because here we have, not a case of *translation*, but of *transference*. Among utterances recorded by Landar *et al.* we have:

(i) č'il bit'aa? nahaló dootl'iž: 'it is bogop like a plant leaf'
(ii) k'os nahaló dootl'iž: 'it is bogop like the sky'
(iii) cédídééh nahaló dootl'iž: 'it is bogop like "purple-four-o'clock" (a flower)'

It is clear (from co-textual evidence) that the appropriate translation equivalents of dootl'iž would be (i) it is *green*, (ii) it is *blue*, and (iii) it is *purple*. These are English lexical items—with formal meanings derived from their membership of an English lexical set, and contextual meanings likewise delimited by the contextual meanings of the other members of the English set. In place of these the form *bogop* is used: this is phonologically and graphologically English—but insofar as it has any formal and contextual meaning, this is derived from membership of a lexical set in Navaho. *Bogop*, is, in fact, the Navaho item dootl'iž fitted up with English phonological/graphological exponents (derived acrophonically from the graphological exponents of the highest-probability English translation equivalents).

6.2   Transference can also be carried out at the level of grammar. In grammatical transference SL grammatical items are represented in the TL text by quasi-TL grammatical items deriving their formal and contextual meanings from the systems and structures of the *SL*, not the TL.

6.21   As an example, we take Indonesian pronouns. Excluding optional (or style-linked) plurals and certain nouns which may function translationwise as equivalents of English pronouns (e.g. the polite *tuan* and *njonja*, and the politically conscious *saudara* 'brother'), Bahasa Indonesia has a nine-term pronoun-system, as opposed to the English seven-term system. Evidently, then, the terms in the two systems have different formal meanings; they have, in addition, different contextual meanings. These differences are approximately indicated in the system-diagrams on the next page.

By superimposing these two system-diagrams we get an indication of translation equivalences: *aku + saja = I, kami + kita =*

Indonesian				*English*	
S	P			S	P
aku / saja	(ex.) kami	(in.) kita	1	I	We
engkau / kamu			2	you	
ia / beliau	mereka		3	he / she / it	they

we, etc. The system-derived 'values', or meanings—formal and contextual—of the items are different; the Indonesian system, for instance, contains two dimensions absent from the English system: *exclusive/inclusive* (kami/kita) and *familiar/non-familiar* (aku/saja, engkau/kamu, ia/beliau—though in this case the 'non-familiar' term, *beliau*, is distinctly honorific). The English system has a *gender* dimension (*he/she/it*), absent in Indonesian; and the extension of *it* and *they* 'downwards', beyond the formal-contextual range of Indonesian pronouns should also be noted.

These diagrams give an approximate indication, as we have said, of translation equivalence; at the same time they indicate that not one English translation equivalent has 'the same meaning' (formally or contextually) as any Indonesian pronoun.

6.22   We can, however, create a quasi-English set of *transference-equivalents*: that is, of items with the formal and contextual meanings of the terms in the Indonesian system. This can be done in several ways: we might press into service the rare or archaic English *thou*, as transference of *engkau*, we might use diacritic letters or numbers, or we might modify the graphological form of English items by adding mnemonically chosen letters: e.g.

-h (non-familiar or (slightly) *h*onorific), -e (*e*xclusive), -i (*i*nclusive). We adopt the last procedure. We can now set up a system of quasi-English pronouns which have (because we have so decided) exactly the same meanings as the Indonesian pronouns[3].

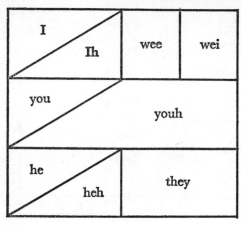

These items *are* in fact, formally and contextually, the Indonesian pronouns; but they are fitted up with English graphological exponents, derived (with arbitrary modifications) from the graphological exponents of the highest-probability English translation equivalents. The transference-equivalents could be embedded in English translations of Indonesian texts and might conceivably be a useful device in teaching the Indonesian use of Indonesian pronouns to English learners; for this purpose the translation might be rank-bound at word rank, true translation equivalents (with English meanings) being used for everything except the pronouns.

6.3   In 'real life' transference is not very common. At first sight, it seems as if the use by a translator of an SL lexical item embedded in a TL text is pure transference. Yet reflection shows (and, in theory, this could be experimentally verified) that an SL lexical item in these circumstances does not fully retain its SL meaning.

[3] Additional quasi-English transference-forms could be found for the bound forms of such Ind. pronouns as have additional forms: e.g. *ku = me*, *-nja = him*, possibly *-mu = youhm*, etc.

6.31 We might, for example, imagine the translator of a Finnish novel rendering the sentence *Menen saunaan* into English as *I'm going to the sauna*. Here, the lexical item *sauna* appears to have been transferred bodily into the TL. Has it, however, taken with it the meaning which it has in Finnish? Certainly not its formal grammatical meaning: probably not its formal lexical meaning nor all of its contextual meaning. For the translator himself, knowing Finnish, it may be that it has its full Finnish meaning; for an English reader it carries a contextual meaning something like 'foreign—specifically Finnish—cultural object or institution somewhat comparable, as the contextual meanings of the co-text show, with the Turkish Bath'—and it is immediately formalized as a (foreign) member of lexical sets containing items like *bath, steambath, Turkish Bath, Public Baths* . . . etc.

6.32 An even better example is the lexical item *sputnik*, which first occurred in English as a 'transference'-item in October 1957. In the co-texts in which it appeared it had the meaning of '(Russian) artificial satellite'—no more. In Russian, of course, the lexical item *sputnik* is a member of a number of lexical sets, and would have an appropriate highest probability English translation equivalent in each: e.g.

> *fellow-traveller* (traveller, wayfarer, companion . . . etc.)
> *companion* (guide to, handbook, introduction)
> *satellite* (planet, earth, moon . . . etc.)
> *(artificial) satellite* (space-ship, rocket . . . etc.)

In English, however, this item was introduced, and has remained, within only the last lexical set, and with the appropriate contextual meaning. Clearly, then, embedded in an English TL text, or, now, simply in an English text, *sputnik* has an English formal and contextual meaning. Since, however, this English meaning of sputnik correlates with *part* of the total *formal-contextual* meaning of Russian *sputnik* we may perhaps speak of *partial transference of meaning*.

6.321 In fact, in the case of *sputnik* four different processes are involved:

(i) *lexical (partial) transference.*

(ii) *grammatical translation:* 'sputnik' as exponent of the Russian

47

UNIVERSITY OF WINDSOR LIBRARY

word-class 'noun' is replaced by 'sputnik' as exponent of the equivalent, but not identical, English word-class 'noun'.

(iii) *phonological translation:* the Russian phonological form / sputn′ik / is replaced by the equivalent English phonological form / sputnik / or / spuᵘtnik / or, with a graphologically derived adaptation, / spətnik /.

(iv) *graphological transliteration:* the Russian form *спутник* is replaced *not* by the English graphological translation equivalent *cnymhuk*, but by the transliteration-equivalent *sputnik*[4].

6.4 Pure meaning-transference may occur when a TL text contains a TL word in its normal TL phonological/graphological form, but with a contextual meaning taken over from the SL. This may happen when one is speaking a foreign language. The Russian who says *My foot hurts*, when he means 'My leg hurts' is using purely English exponents, but transferring the contextual *meaning* of Russian *noga* into an English text. Transferences of this kind occur, though in what is not strictly a translation-situation, in Indian English—for instance in novels about India written in English by Indians. Examples[5] are *government* used, like Hindi *sarkar*, to mean not only the institution of government but also (sp. as a term of address) a person who represents government; *flower-bed*, used by B. Bhattacharya, like Bengali *phul-shajja*, to mean 'nuptial bed'; *brother*, used like Hindi *bhai* both as a kinship term and as a term of address and affection.

6.5 From examples like the foregoing it should be clear that a restricted kind of 'transference of meaning' from one language to another is possible; but it is equally clear that this is not what is normally meant by 'translation'. In *translation*, there is substitution of TL meanings for SL meanings: not transference of SL meanings into the TL. In *transference* there is an *implantation* of SL meanings into the TL text. These two processes must be clearly differentiated in any theory of translation.

---

[4] It sometimes seems a pity that we do not practise graphological translation. Cnymhuk, presumably pronounced / nimhuk /, would be phonaesthetically appropriate!

[5] From B. B. Kachru *An Analysis of Some Features of Indian English: a study in linguistic method.* (Ph.D. thesis, Edinburgh University, 1962.)

7

Conditions of Translation Equivalence

7.1 We are now in a position to consider the necessary conditions in which a given TL item can, or does, function as translation equivalent of a given SL item.

The SL and TL items rarely have 'the same meaning' in the linguistic sense; but they can function in the same situation. In total translation, SL and TL texts or items are translation equivalents when they are *interchangeable in a given situation*. This is why translation equivalence can nearly always be established at sentence-rank—the sentence is the grammatical unit most directly related to speech-function within a situation.

7.2 As our examples in Chapter 5 showed, in total translation SL and TL items have overlapping meanings; their contextual meanings include relationship to certain situational features in common. In the case of Eng. *I have arrived*/Russ. *ja prišla* we saw that even for the rough characterization given in 5.4 we had to specify 8 situational features: 5 for the English text, 6 for the Russian. Only *three* of these (a *speaker*, an *arrival* and a *prior* event) were common to both. The TL text must be relatable to at least *some* of the situational features to which the SL text is relatable. Presumably, the greater the number of situational features common to the contextual meanings of both SL and TL text, the 'better' the translation. The aim in total translation must therefore be to select TL equivalents not with 'the same meaning' as the SL items, but with the greatest possible overlap of situational range. We will return later to the special problems which arise when the situation contains elements relevant to the SL text, but absent from the *cultural context* of the TL.

7.3 In order to generalize our statement of the conditions of translation equivalence so as to be applicable to *restricted* translation as well as *total* translation we must examine these 'situational features' or elements more closely.

7.31   The bundles of situational features which are contextually relevant to a text—that is, those which determine the selection of this or that linguistic form as opposed to any other—are bundles of *distinctive features*; and these are quite analogous to distinctive features in phonology.

Thus, the situational features *arrival*, *prior* event, *linked* to, *present* are situational distinctive features which distinguish the contextual meaning of *have arrived* from that of *have left*, or *arrive*, or *arrived*, or *had arrived*, in much the same way as *stop*, *labial*, *voiceless*, *oral* are distinctive features which distinguish the English phonological unit / p / from / f /, / t /, / b /, / m /.

7.32   Now, the distinctive features of phonology are, in fact, features of *phonic substance*, categorized in general phonetic terms; *general phonetics* being the theory of phonic substance from which we derive descriptive categories ('labial', 'voiceless', etc.) which can be used for describing the distinctive features of phonological units of particular languages. There is, as yet, no general theory of situation-substance, no *general semetics* (or general pleretics)[1] from which to draw descriptive terms for the distinctive features of contextual meanings of grammatical or lexical items in particular languages.

We are therefore forced to operate with *ad hoc* terms in discussing contextual meaning and its relation to situation-substance. But the parallelism holds good; the distinctive features of phonology are phonetically categorized features of phonic substance, the distinctive features of contextual meaning are (semetically categorized) features of situation substance.

7.4   It is now possible to generalize the conditions for translation equivalence as follows:

translation equivalence occurs when an SL and a TL text or item are relatable to (at least some of) the same features of substance.[2]

---

[1] The obvious choice of term is an *-etic* derivate either of *sem-* (from Gk. *sēma*) as in many commonly used terms, or a derivate of *pler-* (from Gk. *plērēs*), as used in Glossematics.

[2] The type of *substance* depends on the *scope* of the translation. For total translation it is situation-substance: for phonological translation it is phonic-substance: for graphological translation it is graphic-substance.

7.41   We can illustrate this from examples already given. The Navaho colour terms referred to in 6.1 above were ico and dootl'iz. If we add icíí we have, very roughly, complete coverage of the visible spectrum. Using the set of English colour terms, Red, Orange, Yellow, Green, Blue, Purple, we can set up an approximate translation-equivalence diagram as follows:

Form:	R	O	Y	G	B	P	English
Substance:	x			y	z		The spectrum
Form:	ɫicíí?	ɫico		dootl'iž			Navaho

The visible spectrum is a continuum of situation-substance. This substantial continuum is dissected and organized into the contextual meanings of English and Navaho linguistic forms roughly as indicated—though, of course, with much less clearcut divisions than are shown here. As we showed in 6.1 the Navaho terms ɫico and dootl'iž (and no doubt also ɫicíí?) do not have the same contextual meanings as any English terms. They are, however, relatable to stretches of the same situation-substance. Let x, y and z represent actual colours present in particular situations, and relatable to the English terms *red, green, blue* occurring in English texts in these situations. The Navaho terms ɫicíí and dootl'iž function as translation equivalents in these situations because they are relatable to the same substantial features x, y and z. It is *solely* this relationship to the same substantial features that justifies their use as translation equivalents since they clearly have quite different meanings from the English items.

7.42   In the same way at the level of grammar, English *we* and Bahasa Indonesia *kami* are translation equivalents in a situation where an English speaker excludes the addressee: e.g. *If you do this, WE will do that.* Here the actual situational features relatable to WE are the *speaker* (S) and at least one *other* (O); the addressee (A) is excluded. Hence the translation equivalence:

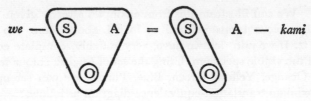

where the outer line in each case indicates the total (potential) system-derived contextual meaning of each item, the inner circle the actual situational elements to which the forms relate.

7.5   We have said that translation equivalence occurs when SL and TL items are relatable to 'the same' features of substance. We will show how this applies in *restricted* translation in Chapters 8 and 9. Meanwhile we must refer to the problems raised by the use here of the term 'the same'.

7.51   In total translation, the question of 'sameness' of situation-substance is a difficult one, and is linked to the question of the 'sameness' or otherwise of the cultures (in the widest and loosest sense) to which SL and TL belong. 'Situation' in relation to contextual meaning, is a wide blanket-term which, within a general semetic theory, requires considerable refinement. Any speech-act takes place in a specific bio-socio-physical environment, at a specific time and place, between specific participants and so on. But the *text* which is (for the linguist) the central item in the speech-act is, or may be, relatable not only to features of this *immediate* situation, but also to features at greater and greater distances (so to speak) reaching out, ultimately, into the total cultural background of the situation. The 'situation', in other words, may be thought of as a series of concentric circles, or spheres, of relevance to the text. Something is said about the relevance of wider or more peripheral situational features in the chapters on *Language Varieties in Translation* and *The Limits of Translatability* (13 and 14 below). Clearly, since translation equivalence demands that SL and TL text should be relatable to 'the same features of substance' there must be community of relevant substance for the two texts.

7.6   Leaving aside the question of total translation, we see that this necessity of 'community of relevant substance' for translation enables us at once to posit the limits of translatability for *restricted* translation. These limits are summed up in two generalizations:

(i) *Translation between media is impossible* (i.e. one cannot 'translate' from the *spoken* to the *written* form of a text or vice-versa).

(ii) *Translation between either of the medium-levels (phonology and graphology) and the levels of grammar and lexis is impossible* (i.e. one cannot 'translate' from SL *phonology* to TL *grammar*, or from SL *lexis* to TL *graphology* . . . etc.).

7.61 These generalizations may require a little elucidation. As to (i): the substance which is relevant to *phonology* is *phonic* substance, and the substance which is relevant to *graphology* is *graphic* substance. The substantial features relevant to a phonological unit or item are sounds produced in a human vocal tract. The substantial features relevant to a graphological unit or item are visible marks on paper, stone . . . etc. Phonic and graphic substance are *absolutely different*; therefore there can be no question of a phonological item being relatable to the same substantial features as a graphological item.

For any particular language, of course, there is an arbitrary relationship between graphological and phonological[3] units. Conversion from spoken to written medium, or vice-versa, is a universal practice among literates; but it is not translation, since it is not replacement by items which are equivalent because of relationship to the same substance.

7.62 For (ii), the same applies: phonic and graphic substance are *absolutely different* from situation-substance. Translations occur in which it looks, at first sight, as if a *phonological* item is being translated by a *grammatical item or items*: e.g. when English: *You're going to Helsinki?* with a final-rise intonation is translated into Finnish as *Menette Helsinkiinkö?* (with falling intonation, but 'interrogative particle' *kö*). Here it may seem as if an English *tone* (a phonological item) has a Finnish *grammatical item* as its translation equivalent. But this is not so. In the SL text, the particular tone is a phonological exponent of the grammatical category 'enquiry' and this in turn has a contextual meaning which relates it to a feature of *situation*-substance. This same feature of

---

[3] Or *formal* units, in the case of what is sometimes called *logographic* writing: e.g. Chinese, Egyptian hieroglyphs.

situation-substance is relatable to the Finnish grammatical category of 'interrogative', whose exponent is *kö/ko*. There is community of substance between SL and TL; but the substance is *situation*-substance for both.

Another—negative—illustration of this is provided by an Anglo-Yiddish joke, from which this is a relevant extract.[4]

A Jew has been accused of horse-stealing, and, in court, the following exchanges take place:

> *Judge:* Did you steal a horse?
> *Interpreter:* Hot ir gestolen a pferd?
> *Accused:* Ikh hob gestolen a ^pferd?
> *Judge:* What did he say?
> *Interpreter:* He said 'I stole a horse'.

The point here is that the interpreter has failed to take note of a feature of the accused's speech: namely, the Yiddish rise-fall tone, ^, which occurs on the word *pferd*. Had he done so, his translation might have been 'What. Me steal a horse?' Now, this looks, at first sight, like failure to translate a *phonological* feature (the rise-fall tone) by a *grammatical* feature (a particular class of clause). But the rise-fall tone is, of course, simply the phonological exponent of a grammatical category of 'incredulity' —and this is relatable to the same situation-substance as is the English clause-class SP, where the exponent of P is an infinitive, or base-form, verbal group.[5]

7.63   There are many other obvious cases where it looks as if a *phonological* feature of an SL text has a *lexical* or *grammatical* equivalent in the TL text. For example, in translation between English and French it may happen that an 'emphatic' '*I* did it.' is translated into French as 'C'est bien moi qui l'ai fait.' Now, it looks, here, as if an English phonological feature—'marked *tonicity*', i.e. a special, contrastive, location of the tonic or tone-bearing foot—is translated 'grammatically' by a special kind of sentence- & clause-structure in French; similarly, 'marked

---

[4] For this example I am indebted to my wife.

[5] On the Yiddish rise-fall tone, cf. Uriel Weinreich, 'On the Yiddish Rise-Fall Intonation Contour', in *For Roman Jakobson*, p. 633.

tonicity' may appear to be translated into Yukagir by special 'assertive' conjugations, marking the Subject, the Predicator or the Complement as major-information-point[6]; again, *vowel-lengthening* in certain Javanese adjectives, translated into English by the use of a (grammatical) 'intensifying sub-modifier', e.g. *terribly, very* . . . etc.

In all these cases, the *phonological* feature (English *tonicity*, Javanese *vowel-lengthening*) is merely the *exponent* of a *grammatical* category; it is this *grammatical* category (not its phonological exponent) which has a grammatical equivalent in the TL.

7.64   There is never any translation from phonology to grammar; nor from *graphology* to grammar. Thus in the first example in the last section *'I did it'* is spoken of as if it represents a certain *phonological* event. But looking at it as a piece of graphology in its own right, we might have suggested that the graphological feature *italicization* of *I* was translated grammatically into French. This, of course, is not so; *italicization* and *tonicity* are simply the corresponding written and spoken exponents of the same grammatical category of major-information-point.

Translation from the levels of grammar and/or lexis to the medium-levels is, of course, equally impossible. If someone says of a given grammatical or lexical item 'this can be translated into English only by the *tone of the voice*' or something of that sort, this must not be taken to mean that an English phonological feature (tone or tonicity) is the translation equivalent of an SL grammatical/lexical feature. It means, simply, that the exponent of the equivalent *grammatical* or *lexical* feature in English happens to be tone or tonicity.

[6] cf. E. A. Kreinovich: *Yukagirskij Yazyk* (Moscow-Leningrad, 1958), pp. 131–38.

8

Phonological Translation

8.1   Phonological translation is restricted translation in which
the SL phonology of a text is replaced by equivalent TL phonology. The grammar and lexis of the SL text remain unchanged,
except insofar as random grammatical or lexical deviations are
entailed in the process. Thus, as mentioned in 2.321 above, the
phonological translation of the English plural 'cats' / kats / into
a language which has no final consonant clusters might be something like / kat /. The phonological translation equivalent here
ends in / t / and thus appears to be a singular.

8.11   The basis for translation equivalence in phonological
translation is relationship of SL and TL phonological units to
'the same' phonic substance. For example, the phonological
translation of English 'had' / had / into Greek is / xent /. The
distinctive phonic substance related to English / h / is 'voiceless
glottal fricative'—i.e. a 'deep' voiceless fricative, that is, one in
which the fricative hiss is generated by turbulent air-flow through
the glottis and modulated by the vocoid-shaping of the mouth.
Greek has only one phoneme related to nearly the same phonic
substance, / x /—i.e. a 'deep' voiceless fricative, the hiss here
being generated by turbulent air-flow through a channel formed
between the dorsal surface of the tongue and the roof of the
mouth, and modulated by the vocoid-shaping of the mouth.
The English / a / is a low front vocoid, and the same phonic
features are present in Gk. / e / (although, in fact, the Gk. vowel
is not so low as the English one—but each is the lowest in the
front series of each language). English / d / is a voiced apical
stop. Gk. has an apical stop / t /, but in Greek the components
'stop' and 'voice' co-occur only when a nasal precedes. The
translation equivalent of English / d / therefore must either be
Greek / t /, or Greek / nt / manifested phonetically as [nd]:
Greeks normally use the latter when speaking English with a
'Greek accent' i.e. in phonological translation.

We may roughly tabulate these relationships in a diagram analogous to that used in 5.43.

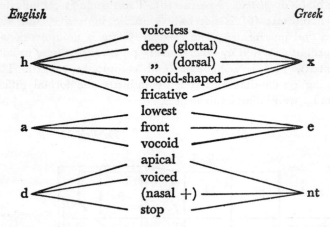

Because Greek has only one vowel in the low front region /e/ as opposed to the two /e, a/ of English, and because of the relation between voicing of stops and a preceding nasal, Greek has a single phonological translation equivalent, /xent/, in phonetic transcription [xɛnd], for the three English phonological forms /hed/ /had/ /hand/.[1]

8.2   In phonological translation, as in translation at other levels, one must distinguish between formal correspondence and translation equivalence. We may take as an example a small sub-system of phonemes, *labial stops* in English and Sindhi. The English system is one of two terms / p / and / b /; the Sindhi system is one of five terms / p / / ph / / b / / bh / / ɓ /. Formally, then, there can be no correspondence between the English and Sindhi terms. It is possible, however, to set up *translation equivalences* by considering the features of phonic substance to which the English and Sindhi phonological units are related. In terms of distinctive phonic features the Sindhi system is

---

[1] A fact which is very troublesome for Greek beginners in English, the situation being further complicated, as D. Abercrombie has pointed out (*Problems and Principles*, Longmans Green, 1956, pp. 11 and 26) by the fact that the modern Greek χέρι is a *lexical* translation-equivalent of English *arm* as well as *hand*.

3-dimensional; each term is either *unaspirated* (p b 6) or *aspirated* (ph bh), *voiceless* (p ph) or *voiced* (b bh 6), *pulmonic egressive* (p ph b bh) or *glottalic ingressive* (6). The system is complicated by syncretisms: (6) is not only glottalic ingressive, but also voiced and unaspirated. The English system is unidimensional, again slightly skewed by syncretisms; / p / is *voiceless* (and usually aspirated), / b / is *unaspirated* (and commonly voiced). The following system-diagrams roughly indicate the formal differences and translation equivalences.

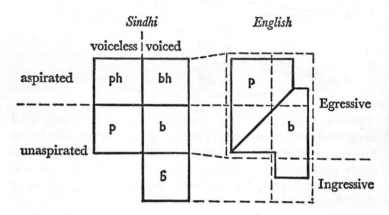

The dotted outline of the English system-diagram indicates the limits, in phonic substance, of the Sindhi system—limits rarely, if ever, reached by the English phonemes; on the other hand, English / b / is shown as extending into the phonic-substance areas of Sindhi / p / / 6 / and / bh /. In general, superimposition of the two diagrams roughly indicates both the non-correspondence of the phonological systems, and the possibilities of translation equivalence.

8.21 The normal Sindhi translation equivalent of English / b / is Sindhi / b / since both are related to *voice* and *unaspirated* as features of phonic substance. However, English / b / can, on occasion, be *voiceless unaspirated*, or realized as a weak *glottalic ingressive*, or followed by a 'whispery-voiced' vowel (i.e. be '*voiced aspirated*'); there may thus be occasions when the Sindhi translation equivalent of Eng. / b / may be / p /, / 6 / or / bh /. In other words, we can say 'the highest probability Sindhi translation equivalent of Eng. / b / is / b /; but in special co-textual conditions other equivalents may occur'. And, by taking note of the special factors involved we could, in theory, determine the conditioned probabilities of these equivalences.

8.3 Phonological translation is thus seen to parallel 'total translation' quite closely; for any one SL phonological item there may be more than one TL phonological translation equivalent. The particular TL equivalent depends on what particular features of phonic substance are relatable to the SL item on that particular occasion; precisely as the particular English translation equivalent of Navaho dootl'iž depends on what specific feature of situation-substance (what colour) is relatable to the Navaho item on that occasion.

8.4 Phonological translation, like total translation, may involve change of rank, or regrouping and reorganizing of features of substance into the formal units of the TL. For example, in phonological translation between English and Japanese, equivalence often has to be established not merely at *phoneme* rank, but with an upward change of rank, to the next higher unit in the Japanese phonological hierarchy—namely the *mora* or 'kana' (somewhat similar to, though neither formally nor substantially identical with the English *syllable*). Thus English *platonic love*, phonologically (ignoring, for the present, anything above the phoneme rank in English) / plᵊtonik lᵊv / has as its Japanese phonological translation equivalent / puratonikkurabu /.

8.41 We may show the translation equivalences here as follows:

English   p lᵊ to ni k   lə v
Japanese pu ra to ni k-ku ra bu

The English phonemes / p / and / v / have, as Japanese translation equivalents, the morae / pu / and / bu /; and the phoneme / k / has, as its translation equivalent, two Japanese morae / k-ku /. The reason for these equivalences is that, except in certain definable circumstances, the Japanese mora always has the structure CV; an English C before C, or finally, is thus normally represented by a Japanese CV structure. Moreover, the Japanese high vowels / u / and / i / are often realized *voiceless* or as phonic *zero*; hence / pu-ra / is most nearly relatable to the same phonic substance as English / pl /, with the 'aspiration' of / p / manifested phonically as a partially voiceless / l /.

The equivalence / k / = / k-ku / requires further comment. Here the Japanese translation treats, as phonologically relevant, a feature which is present in the phonic substance of the English utterance—namely, *length* of / k / after a short vowel—but is not phonologically relevant in English. This is precisely paralleled in total translation by, for example, Russian treating a situational feature (*on foot*) as linguistically relevant in *prišla* for English *have arrived* (see 5.4 above).

8.5   Another example of the reorganization of phonic substance into TL phonological units which may occur in phonological translation is provided by the following true story[2].

A Scotsman in France went to buy an ice-cream cone at a kiosk. Two types were available—one with a single ball of ice-cream, the other with two balls of ice-cream side by side. The Scotsman wanted one of these double helpings, so he asked in English, for 'a double'. He was unhesitatingly served with the type required.

8.51   Assuming that the ice-cream vendor was monolingual (which is almost certain) what happened was probably this: the English / dəbl / (with a 'dark', or strongly velarized / l / was 'translated' at the phonological level into / dø bul /, and interpreted by the vendor as 'deux boules'—the correct French technical term for the type of ice-cream required.

The similarity of phonic substance justifying the translation equivalence of French / d /, / b / to English / d /, / b / requires no comment. The equivalence / ə / = / ø / is easily explained; the phonic substance: 'obscure (i.e. not clearly front-unrounded or back rounded) or "mixed" vocoid' is common to / ə / and / ø /. The explanation of / l / = / ul / is more interesting. Here the phonic features '*laterality*' and '*velarity*', simultaneously present in the phonic substance of English / l / are redistributed in translation into a sequence of two phonemes: / u / (incorporating velarity) and / l / (incorporating laterality).

[2] I am indebted to my colleague J. McH. Sinclair for this example.

A parallel in total translation would again be the translation of Russian *prišla* by *arrived on foot*; here a feature of situation substance which is related to the single lexical item PRIITI in Russian must, if incorporated into the English translation at all, be redistributed as indicated.

8.6 Phonological translation, as we remarked in 2.323, is practised deliberately by actors and mimics when they assume a foreign, or dialectal, pronunciation. It can occur, receptively, as in the example just given, and it occurs productively, though inadvertently, in the imperfect pronunciation of someone speaking a foreign language. We usually call this latter 'phonological (or phonetic) interference' and think of it as a transference of native (L_1) phonology *into* the foreign language (L_2) being spoken. This is a perfectly possible way of describing the phenomenon. From the point of view of translation-theory, however, it may be regarded as translation *from* the L_2 into the L_1, at the phonological level only, since it is replacement of L_2 phonology by equivalent L_1 phonology (lexis and grammar remaining unchanged).

In normal total translation the SL phonology is not translated, but merely *replaced* by whatever (non-equivalent) TL phonology is entailed by the selection of TL grammatical and lexical items. In certain circumstances, however, the translator attempts to reproduce at least *some* features of SL phonology in the TL text—i.e. performs a partial phonological translation, and this, in turn, affects the grammatical/lexical translation, since the selection of translation equivalents at these formal levels is partly determined by the need for their phonological exponents to be translation equivalents of phonological items in the SL. This happens typically in *film-dubbing*, where the translator may select lexical translation equivalents in the TL which have *labials*, for instance, in their phonological forms, to match labials in the phonological forms of the SL items. In the translation of poetry, too, some attempt may be made to select TL equivalents which 'match the sound' of SL items; this entails some degree of phonological translation.

9

Graphological Translation

9.1   Graphological translation is restricted translation in which the SL graphology of a text is replaced by equivalent TL graphology. The basis for equivalence is relationship to 'the same' graphic substance.

The discussion of graphological translation is more difficult than the discussion of phonological translation because we have no systematic theory of graphic substance—no 'general graphetics'—from which to draw categories for the description of graphic substance. We therefore construct 'graphetic categories' *ad hoc* for the present section.

9.2   We can illustrate graphological translation fairly simply by means of the Cyrillic and Roman alphabets. To simplify the discussion still further, we will confine ourselves to capitals.

9.21   On the basis of a rough graphetic analysis, we can say that the graphological units, or letters, of the two alphabets make use of eight distinctive features of graphic substance, subject to certain systematic modifications. These are: *vertical* | , *horizontal* —, *right oblique* / , *right oblique curved* ⌐ , *left oblique* \ , *right semicircle* ⊃ , *left semicircle* ⊂ , *supine semicircle* ∪.

The modifications are: *full* | / — ⊃ etc., *low* ₁/₋⊃ etc., *high* ¹/⁻⊃ etc. and (for __ only) *mid*—. Full can be unmarked: other modifications indicated by *l, h, m*. (An additional modification, *reduced* (r) is occasionally useful.)

Finally, there are categories of combination, e.g. (a) *attached*, (x) *crossing*, (c) *connecting*. If graphic features are named in a sequence corresponding to *left-to-right*, and *upwards* for ascenders (verticals and obliques), attachment points can usually be left undescribed, and normal end-attachment can be assumed except when otherwise stated.

Thus, in both Cyrillic and Roman we have, for instance:

A = / \ — mc	B = | ⊃ h ⊃ l
H = | | — mc	T = | — hx
X = / \ x	K = | / h \ l

For Cyrillic only:

Б = | ‿ h ⊃ 1   Г = | — h
И = | | / c   Л = ⌐ — hr |
Д = ⌐ — hr | — 1 | lra | lra Ж = ⊃ | ⊂ — mc
                        [or Ж = (| / \ ) x]

9.22   The appropriate graphological translation equivalents are, in many cases, obvious. The following Cyrillic letters, however, present problems:

Б Г Д Ж З Л П У Ф Ц Ч Ш Щ Ъ Ы Ь Э Ю Я

9.23   We shall analyse a few in detail.
Б: distinctive features: | — h ⊃ 1: i.e., counting modifications, 5 features.
Several Roman letters have 2 or 3 features in common:

D (| ⊃), T (| — hx), F (| — h — m), B (| ⊃ h ⊃ 1).

The attachment point of the high horizontal in T ('crossing') tends to rule T out. The choice lies between F and B, both of which have 3 features in common with Б . We decide, somewhat arbitrarily or impressionistically, for B.

Г: | — h Possible translation equivalents: L (| — 1), F (| — h — m), T (| — hx). F has all three features of Г, L has only two. However, F introduces two additional features (— and m). We therefore choose L.

Д: ⌐ | — hrc — lc | lra | lra No close equivalent. Best is possibly A, which, like Д, has two ascenders, and a horizontal connector. But Д is almost untranslatable.

Ж: ⊃ | ⊂ — mxc No close equivalent. Redistribution into two letters is almost essential. DC is possible, this has 3 features in common (| ⊃ ⊂), though rearranged. HC (| | — mc, ⊂) has 4 common features. We select HC.

З : ⊃ h ⊃ 1 Only possible equivalent: S (⊂ h ⊃ 1)

Л : ⌐ — hrc | No single letter equivalent. Best approximation is JT (⌣ | , | — hx)

9.24   We summarize the rest:

П (| — hc |) = H (| — mc |),
У (\ h ⌡) = Y (\ h / h | l),
Ф (⊂ ⊃ | x) = Q (⊂ ⊃ | xlr),
Ц (| — lc |) = U (| ∪ lc |),
Ч (∪ h |) = J (∪ | |),
Ш (| | | — lc)—no near equivalent; use W (\/ 1 \1/),
Щ (| | | — lc) | lr)— useW, Э (⊃ — m) = D (⊃ |),
Ю (| — mrc ⊂ ⊃) = IO, Я (/ 1 ⊂ h |) = R (| ⊃ h \ l).

Ы | and Ь are difficult. No Roman letter has 'low reduced right semicircle'. Ignoring this we can translate Ы as II, Ь as I (if lower-case were used, the equivalents would be bl and l). Ъ can only be T or Z. Neither is very close: we choose Z.

9.3   Here, again, in graphological translation, we see that phenomena analogous to those of total translation occur. First, the TL equivalent is seldom related to exactly the same set of substance-features as the SL item. Secondly a single unit of SL may have to be redistributed into two TL units.

9.31   The following is an example of graphological translation from Russian (Cyrillic) into Roman caps.

ЖЕЛЕЗНАЯ ДОРОГА = HCEJTESHAR AOPOLA
СПУТНИК = CHYTHNK

9.32   Above we gave a graphological translation of *sputnik* from Russian italic, or cursive, (*спутник*) as *спутник*. This, again, illustrates a phenomenon found in total translation. The difference between caps. and lower-case is one of medium-variety, and is thus more or less equivalent to a difference at the grammatical/ lexical levels between dialects, registers or styles. Different varieties, of course, have different characteristics and call for different TL equivalents.

9.4   Graphological translation is often particularly difficult because writing systems tend to make use of a restricted range of graphic substance; the straight lines and sharp angles of Armenian script, for instance, have little substance in common with the curves and circles of Burmese, or some South Indian scripts.

Occasionally one can make some degree of graphological translation between mutually exotic scripts, but this is often limited in extent. The following, for instance, is a graphological translation from a cursive Roman into Arabic:

$$\textit{Arabic} \qquad \textit{Arabic}$$

The translation does some slight violence to Arabic writing conventions, but apart from that, the translation equivalences can all be justified by relation of English and Arabic letters to similar features of graphic substance.

9.5   An approximation to graphological translation is occasionally practised deliberately by typographers who wish to give an 'exotic' flavour to written texts. For example, books about Islam or the Arab world sometimes have their titles written in somewhat Arabic-looking script—a graphological semi-translation.

Persons writing in a foreign language may occasionally produce graphological translations; for example, Greeks writing in English (or in Roman in general) often replace a script a by α, or an n by η. It is particularly clear in the case of η for n that this is graphological translation, since the only thing in common between n and η is relation to similar graphic substance.

10

Transliteration

10.1　It will now be clear that graphological translation is quite different from *transliteration*. We repeat here an example from 9.31 with a transliteration added.

Original:	СПУТНИК
Graphological Translation:	CHYTHNK
Transliteration:	SPUTNIK

In transliteration, SL graphological units are replaced by TL graphological units; but these are not translation equivalents, since they are not selected on the basis of relationship to the same graphic substance.

In the process of actually transliterating a text, the transliterator replaces each SL letter or other graphological unit by a TL letter, or other unit, on the basis of a conventionally established set of rules. The transliteration rules specify transliteration-equivalents which differ from translation equivalents in two ways: first, in not necessarily being relatable to the same graphic substance as the SL letters; secondly, in being (in good transliteration) in *one-to-one correspondence* with SL letters or other units.

10.2　In principle, the process of setting up a transliteration-system involves three steps:

(i) SL letters are replaced by SL phonological units; this is the normal literate process of converting from the written to the spoken medium.

(ii) The SL phonological units are translated into TL phonological units.

(iii) The TL phonological units are converted into TL letters, or other graphological units.

In a simplified way this process may be indicated as follows. Transliteration here is from Russian into English.

	SL graph. units	SL phon. units	=	TL phon. units	TL graph. units
1.	Б	/b/	=	/b/	B
2.	В	/v/	=	/v/	V
3.	Ч	/tʃ/	=	/tʃ/	CH
4.	Х	/x/	=	/h/	H etc.

This table is to be interpreted thus: in 1. the Russian (Cyrillic) graphological unit Б is convertible into the Russian phonological unit /b/. This /b/ has phonic features (voice, labiality, stopness) in common with the English phonological unit /b/, hence English /b/ is its English phonological translation equivalent. The English phonological unit /b/ is convertible into the English graphological unit B. The letter B is thus the English *transliteration equivalent* of the Russian Б. In 3. we have a single Russian letter Ч with its phonological counterpart /tʃ/. The English phonological translation equivalent is /tʃ/, but this has no single letter exponent in English graphology—it is convertible to CH. Hence the English letter-sequence CH is the transliteration-equivalent of the Russian single letter Ч.

10.3   There are, however, several complicating factors.

(i) A given SL letter may have more than one SL phonological correspondent. In this case only *one* of these must be chosen as basis for transliteration: e.g. in transliteration from English into Russian we could find that Eng. C → either / k / or / s /. For Russian transliteration equivalent we should have to choose between the Cyrillic letters K and C.

(ii) In phonological translation between SL and TL there may not be—indeed normally is not—one-to-one equivalence between SL and TL phonological units; where two or more SL units have the same TL phonological translation equivalent an arbitrary distinction must be introduced into the TL graphological representation of these units. For example, in transliteration from Sanskrit (Devanagari) into Roman (say, English) we would find the following situation:

SL graph. units	SL phon. units	TL phon. unit	TL graph. unit	
श⟶	/ʃ/ ⎫			SH
ष⟶	/ʂ/ ⎭ = /ʃ/	SH, arbitrarily split ⟶		*SH*

(iii) In converting from TL phonological to graphological units there may be a selection of letters to choose from; a decision must be made arbitrarily.

Thus, in transliterating, say, Russian К into English we can set up the phonological translation equivalent /k/ = /k/. We then have to choose between converting /k/ → K or → C. We might make an arbitrary choice, say C. Or we might decide to transliterate К by K, thus releasing C as the transliteration equivalent of Ц.

10.4   A particular complication arises when the TL graphological units are not immediately convertible to TL phonological units. This happens in languages where the writing system is 'logographic'[1], e.g. Chinese. The Chinese graphological unit—the *character*—is directly convertible to a lexical or grammatical unit of the language. 'Transliteration' in such a case can only be through the phonological form of the lexical or grammatical unit associated with the character.

In other words, given the character 人 we can 'transliterate' into English only by first converting the character 人 into the lexical item which it represents, and then 'transliterating' that as, say, *ren*. But this is not transliteration, in that the graphological units of the TL form are not in one-to-one correlation with graphological units of the SL. It is, on the contrary, a form of *transcription* (see 10.6 below).

10.5   One final complication must be mentioned. Transliteration is a conventionalized process, unlike translation which is carried out anew, or *ad hoc*, on each particular occasion. In transliteration, what we have so far called the 'TL' may not, strictly, be a 'language' (or the writing system of a specific language) at all.

Thus, for example, the traditional transliteration of Sanskrit is into Roman letters—but it is not, strictly, into Latin graphology, for the Roman alphabet has to be supplemented by a number of diacritics to correspond to letter-distinctions in Skt. which are not present in Latin.

10.6   In 10.4 above we mentioned *transcription*. A *transcription* is

---

[1] Often erroneously called 'ideographic' or 'pictographic'.

a writing-system in which the letters or graphological units are in one-to-one correlation with phonological units—or with spans or segments of phonic substance. In the first case we have a *phonological* transcription (which may be *phonemic, allophonic, prosodic,* etc.) and in the second, a *phonetic* transcription.

The distinction between transliteration and transcription is important, and often misunderstood. For example, it has been argued that Hebrew cannot be 'Romanized' because Romanization distorts the language; i.e. fails to show the formal and phonological relatedness of lexically or grammatically related forms.

The source of this contention is the fact that it is tacitly assumed that a Romanized writing system for Hebrew will necessarily be a phonemic transcription. Now, a phonemic transcription of Hebrew may, indeed, do precisely what is feared; to understand why, one must remember that the Hebrew script, like the Arabic script, is basically syllabic. Each letter represents, essentially, a specific consonant, with the implication of a following (unspecified) vowel. The particular vowel can, if desired, be indicated by a diacritic mark; in addition, suppression of the implied vowel can also be marked. Moreover, certain letters represent (syllables beginning with) consonants which alternate between a *stop* and a *fricative* stricture-type.

In traditional Hebrew orthography the 'consonantal shape' of a lexical item is preserved throughout its paradigmatic morphological changes, because the varying vowels, and the consonantal alternations, are either not graphically represented, or represented only by diacritics; thus, for the verb 'to write' we have the following forms:

Infin.	*Imper.*	*3rd sg. past*	*present*	etc.
לכתב	כתב	כתב	כותב	etc.

In transcription:

lixtov	ktov	katav	kōtēv	etc.

But, in true transliteration:

lktb	ktb	ktb	kwtb

or, with diacritic vowels:

$$l^ikt^ob \qquad kt^ob \qquad k^at^ab \qquad k^\bar{o}wt^\bar{e}b$$

Transcription is a representation of phonological units: *transliteration*, however, gives a one-to-one representation of graphological units, and consequently can represent precisely the traditional Hebrew orthography, and preserve the visual relatedness between forms, which a phonemic transcription tends to obscure.

11

Grammatical and Lexical Translation

11.1 *Grammatical translation* is restricted translation in which the SL grammar of a text is replaced by equivalent TL grammar, but with no replacement of lexis. The basis for equivalence here, as in total translation, is relationship to the same situation-substance.

11.11 Thus, given an English SL text such as *This is the man I saw*, we might translate it *grammatically* into French as *Voici le man que j'ai see-é*: or into Arabic as *haada 'l-man 'ili see-t-u*. In both of these translations we have retained the two lexical items, *man* and *see*, unchanged, but have replaced all the grammatical items by equivalent French or Arabic grammatical items.

11.12 In more detail, the process of grammatical translation in the Arabic example is as follows:

English clause-structure *SPC* = Arabic *SPC* or *SC*; the latter being translation equivalent of an English SPC structure in which P = *be* (present tense), as here. So here we have SPC = SC.

The exponent of S in the English text is the item *this*, a term in the system of English deictics; the Arabic translation equivalent is *haada*. The exponent of C in English is the Ngp *the man I saw*, i.e. a Ngp with the structure MHQ in which the exponent of M is the *definite article* the for which the Arabic translation equivalent is *al*. The exponent of H is the lexical item *man*, which remains unchanged. The exponent of Q is a rank-shifted clause of structure SP. The Arabic equivalent is a rank-shifted clause of structure ᶜAˢᵖᶜ i.e. with connective ᶜA ('ili) and a complex predicator with bound subject-object morphemes: (an approximate morpheme-rank-bound total back-translation of the Arabic C would be *the man which see-d-I-him*).

Hence the grammatical translation:

Haada al-man 'ili see-t-u.

11.2 *Lexical translation* is restricted translation in which the SL lexis of a text is replaced by equivalent TL lexis, but with no replacement of grammar. The basis of equivalence again is relationship to the same situation-substance.

11.21   Thus our same text, *This is the man I saw*, translated *lexically* into French and Arabic would be: Fr. *This is the homme I voi-ed* and *This is the rajul I shuf-ed*.

11.22   Here, the English SL grammar is preserved, but the lexical items man and see are replaced by the equivalent TL items *homme/rajul* and *voi-/shuf*.

11.23   Now it is at once evident that, unlike grammatical translation, this process, or one very like it, occurs in real life. British soldiers in the Middle East have often produced utterances not unlike 'This is the rajul I shufed'. In other words, the process of 'picking up a few words' of the language, and then throwing them into utterances in the speaker's primary language involves lexical translation—rarely, if ever, grammatical translation.

11.3   Since grammar and lexis between them exhaust the formal levels of language, grammatical and lexical translation between any two languages are the converse of each other; that is to say, *grammatical* translation from language A into language B is the same as *lexical* translation from language B into language A.

The following diagram shows the relations between grammatical, lexical, and total translation:

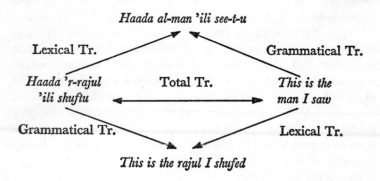

12

Translation Shifts

HAVING reviewed all types of restricted translation we return, now, to general discussion; in particular, to a brief systematic survey of some of the changes or 'shifts' which occur in translation. By 'shifts' we mean departures from formal correspondence in the process of going from the SL to the TL. Two major types of 'shift' occur: *level shifts* (12.1) and *category shifts* (12.2).

12.1 *Level shifts.* By a shift of level we mean that a SL item at one linguistic level has a TL translation equivalent at a different level.

We have already pointed out (7.6) that translation between the levels of phonology and graphology—or between either of these levels and the levels of grammar and lexis—is impossible. Translation between these levels is absolutely ruled out by our theory, which posits 'relationship to the same substance' as the necessary condition of translation equivalence. We are left, then, with shifts from *grammar* to *lexis* and vice-versa as the only possible level-shifts in translation; and such shifts are, of course, quite common.

12.11 Examples of level shifts are sometimes encountered in the translation of the verbal aspects of Russian and English. Both these languages have an aspectual opposition—of very roughly the same type—seen most clearly in the 'past' or *preterite* tense: the opposition between Russian *imperfective* and *perfective* (e.g. *pisal* and *napisal*), and between English *simple* and *continuous* (*wrote* and *was writing*).

There is, however, an important difference between the two aspect systems, namely that the *polarity of marking* is not the same. In Russian, the (contextually) marked term in the system is the *perfective*; this explicitly refers to the *uniqueness* or *completion* of the event. The *imperfective* is unmarked—in other words it is relatively neutral in these respects (the event may or may not actually be unique or completed, etc., but at any rate the imperfective is indifferent to these features—does not explicitly refer to this 'perfectiveness').[1]

In English, the (contextually and morphologically) marked term is the *continuous*; this explicitly refers to the development, the *progress*, of the event. The 'simple' form is neutral in this respect (the event may or may not actually be in progress, but the simple form does not explicitly refer to this aspect of the event).

We indicate these differences in the following diagram, in which the marked terms in the Russian and English aspect-systems are enclosed in rectangles:

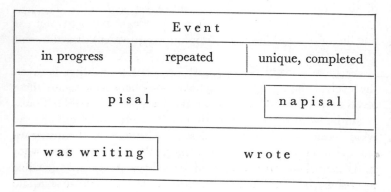

12.12   One result of this difference between Russian and English is that Russian *imperfective* (e.g. pisal) is translatable with almost equal frequency by English *simple* (wrote) or *continuous* (was writing). But the *marked* terms (napisal—was writing) are mutually untranslatable.

A Russian writer can create a certain contrastive effect by using an imperfective and then, so to speak, 'capping' this by using the (marked) perfective. In such a case, the same effect of explicit, contrastive, reference to *completion* may have to be translated into English by a change of lexical item. The following example[2] shows this:

---

[1] My attention was first drawn to this difference between English and Russian by Roman Jakobson in a lecture which he gave in London in 1950.

[2] From *Herzen*, cited by *Unbegaun* in Grammaire Russe, p. 217.

'Čto že *delal* Bel'tov v prodolženie etix des'ati let? Vse il počti vse. Čto on *sdelal*? Ničego ili počti ničego.'

Here the imperfective, *delal*, is 'capped' by the perfective *sdelal*. *delal* can be translated by either *did* or *was doing*—but, since there is no contextual reason to make explicit reference to the *progress* of the event, the former is the better translation. We can thus say 'What *did* Beltov *do* . . .?' The Russian perfective, with its marked insistence on *completion* can cap this effectively: 'What did he *do and complete*?' But the English marked term insists on the *progress* of the event, so cannot be used here. ('What *was* he *doing*' is obviously inappropriate.) In English, in this case, we must use a different lexical verb: a *lexical* item which includes reference to completion in its contextual meaning, e.g. *achieve*[3]. The whole passage can thus be translated:

'What did Beltov do during these ten years? Everything, or almost everything. What did he achieve? Nothing, or almost nothing.'

12.13   Cases of more or less incomplete shift from grammar to lexis are quite frequent in translation between other languages. For example, the English: *This text is intended for* . . . may have as its French TL equivalent: *Le présent Manuel s'adresse à.* . . . Here the SL modifier, *This*—a term in a *grammatical* system of deictics—has as its TL equivalent the modifier *Le présent*, an article + a lexical adjective. Such cases are not rare in French, cf. also *This may reach you before I arrive* = Fr. *Il se peut que ce mot vous parvienne avant mon arrivée.* Once again the grammatical item *this* has a partially lexical translation equivalent *ce mot*.[4]

12.2   *Category shifts.* In 2.4 we referred to *unbounded* and *rankbound* translation: the first being approximately 'normal' or 'free' translation in which SL-TL equivalences are set up at whatever rank is appropriate. Usually, but not always, there is sentence-

---

[3] Another possibility would be 'What *did* he *get done*?', but this would be stylistically less satisfactory.

[4] Examples from Vinay et Darbelnet, *Stylistique Comparée du français et de l'anglais*, p. 99.

UNIVERSITY OF WINDSOR LIBRARY 75

sentence equivalence[5], but in the course of a text, equivalences may shift up and down the rank-scale, often being established at ranks lower than the sentence. We use the term 'rank-bound' translation only to refer to those special cases where equivalence is *deliberately limited* to ranks below the sentence, thus leading to 'bad translation' = i.e. translation in which the TL text is either not a normal TL form at all, or is not relatable to the same situational substance as the SL text.

In normal, unbounded, translation, then, translation equivalences may occur between sentences, clauses, groups, words and (though rarely) morphemes. The following is an example where equivalence can be established to some extent right down to morpheme rank:

Fr. SL text J'ai laissé mes lunettes sur la table
Eng. TL text I've left my glasses on the table

Not infrequently, however, one cannot set up simple equal-rank equivalence between SL and TL texts. An SL *group* may have a TL *clause* as its translation equivalent, and so on.

Changes of rank (unit-shifts) are by no means the only changes of this type which occur in translation; there are also changes of *structure*, changes of *class*, changes of *term* in systems, etc. Some of these—particularly *structure-changes*—are even more frequent than rank-changes.

It is changes of these types which we refer to as *category-shifts*. The concept of 'category-shift' is necessary in the discussion of translation; but it is clearly meaningless to talk about category-shift unless we assume some degree of formal correspondence between SL and TL; indeed this is the main justification for the recognition of formal correspondence in our theory (cf. Chapter 4). Category-shifts are *departures from formal correspondence* in translation.

We give here a brief discussion and illustration of category-shifts, in the order *structure-shifts*, *class-shifts*, *unit-shifts* (rank-changes), *intra-system-shifts*.

[5] W. Freeman Twaddell has drawn my attention to the fact that in German-English translation, equivalence may be rather frequently established between the German *sentence* and an English unit greater than the sentence, e.g. *paragraph*.

12.21 *Structure-shifts.* These are amongst the most frequent category shifts at all ranks in translation; they occur in *phonological* and *graphological* translation as well as in *total translation.*

12.211 In *grammar*, structure-shifts can occur at all ranks. The following English-Gaelic instance is an example of *clause-structure shift.*

| SL text | *John loves Mary* | = SPC |
| TL text | *Tha gradh aig Iain air Mairi* | = PSCA |

(A rank-bound word-word back-translation of the Gaelic TL text gives us: *Is love at John on Mary*)

We can regard this as a structure-shift only on the assumption that there is formal correspondence between English and Gaelic. We must posit that the English elements of clause-structure S, P, C, A have formal correspondents S, P, C, A in Gaelic; this assumption appears reasonable, and so entitles us to say that a Gaelic PSCA structure as translation equivalent of English SPC represents a *structure-shift* insofar as it contains different elements.

But the Gaelic clause not only contains different elements—it also places two of these (S and P) in a different sequence. Now, if the sequence $\overrightarrow{SP}$ were the only possible sequence in English (as $\overrightarrow{PS}$ is in Gaelic) we could ignore the *sequence* and, looking only at the particular elements, S and P, say that the English and Gaelic structures were the same as far as *occurrence* in them of S and P was concerned. But sequence *is* relevant in English and we therefore count it as a feature of the structure, and say that, in this respect, too, structure-shift occurs in the translation.

12.212 Another pair of examples will make this point clearer by contrasting a case where structure-shift occurs with one where it does not.

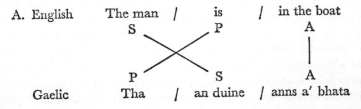

77

and

B. English   Is   /   the man   /   in the boat?

$$P \qquad\qquad S \qquad\qquad A$$
$$| \qquad\qquad | \qquad\qquad |$$
$$P \qquad\qquad S \qquad\qquad A$$

Gaelic   Am bheil / an duine   / anns a' bhata?

In B, there is complete formal correspondence of clause-structure (no structure-shift): in A, there is a structure-shift at clause-rank.

These two examples, in fact, provide us with a commutation which establishes the following translation equivalences:

A.   English $\overrightarrow{(SP)}$ Gaelic V^A at P

B.   English $\overleftarrow{(SP)}$ Gaelic V^I at P

In other words, the Gaelic translation equivalent of the English sequence → of S and P in clause-structure is the occurrence in Gaelic of a verbal group of the class *Affirmative* as exponent of P; the Gaelic translation equivalent of the English sequence ← of S and P in clause-structure is the occurrence in Gaelic of a verbal group of the class *Interrogative* as exponent of P.

These two examples in fact illustrate two different types of translation-shift; in A, there is structure-shift; in B, there is unit-shift, since in this case the Gaelic equivalent of a feature at *clause*-rank is the selection of a particular term in a system operating at *group* rank.

12.213   Structure-shifts can be found at other ranks, for example at group rank. In translation between English and French, for instance, there is often a shift from MH (modifier + head) to (M)HQ ((modifier +) head + qualifier), e.g. *A white house* (MH) = *Une maison blanche* (MHQ).

12.22   *Class-shifts.* Following Halliday, we define a *class* as 'that grouping of members of a given unit which is defined by operation in the structure of the unit next above'. Class-shift, then, occurs when the translation equivalent of a SL item is a member of a different class from the original item. Because of the logical dependence of class on structure (of the unit at the rank above) it is clear that structure-shifts usually entail class-shifts, though this may be demonstrable only at a secondary degree of delicacy.

For example, in the example given in 12.213 above (*a white house = une maison blanche*), the translation equivalent of the English *adjective* 'white' is the French adjective 'blanche'. Insofar as both 'white' and 'blanche' are exponents of the formally corresponding class *adjective* there is apparently no class-shift. However, at a further degree of delicacy we may recognize two sub-classes of adjectives; those operating at M and those operating at Q in Ngp structure. (Q-adjectives are numerous in French, very rare in English.) Since English 'white' is an M-adjective and French 'blanche' is a Q-adjective it is clear that the shift from M to Q entails a class-shift.

In other cases, also exemplified in the translation of Ngps from English to French and vice-versa, class-shifts are more obvious: e.g. Eng. *a medical student = Fr. un étudiant en médecine*. Here the translation equivalent of the adjective *medical*, operating at M, is the adverbial phrase *en médecine*, operating at Q; and the lexical equivalent of the adjective *medical* is the noun *médecine*.

12.23   *Unit-shift.* By unit-shift we mean changes of rank—that is, departures from formal correspondence in which the translation equivalent of a unit at one rank in the SL is a unit at a different rank in the TL.

We have already seen several examples of unit shift in what precedes: e.g. in sections 3.222, 3.223, 8.41, 12.211, 12.213. A more appropriate term might be 'rank-shift', but since this has been assigned a different, technical, meaning within Halliday's theory of grammar we cannot use it here.

12.24   *Intra-system shift.* In a listing of types of translation-shift, such as we gave in 12.2 above, one might expect 'system-shift' to occur along with the names of the types of shift affecting the other fundamental categories of grammar—unit, structure and class. There is a good reason for not naming one of our types of shift 'system-shift', since this could only mean a departure from formal correspondence in which (a term operating in) one system in the SL has as its translation equivalent (a term operating in) a different—non-corresponding—system in the TL. Clearly, however, such shifts from one *system* to another are always entailed by unit-shift or class-shift. For instance, in example B in 12.212

the Gaelic equivalent of English clause-structure *PS* is shown to be selection of a particular class of Verbal group (V^I). We could say that here there is a system-shift, since PS, a term in a system of clause-classes, is replaced by V^I, a term in a (formally non-corresponding) system of Vgp classes. There is no need to do this, however, since such a shift is already implied by the *unit-shift*.

We use the term *intra-system shift* for those cases where the shift occurs *internally*, within a system; that is, for those cases where SL and TL possess systems which approximately correspond formally as to their constitution, but when translation involves selection of a non-corresponding term in the TL system.

It may, for example, be said that English and French possess formally corresponding systems of *number*. In each language, the system operates in *nominal groups*, and is characterized by concord between the exponents of S and P in clauses and so on. Moreover, in each language, the system is one of two terms—*singular* and *plural*—and these terms may also be regarded as formally corresponding. The exponents of the terms are differently distributed in the two languages—e.g. Eng. *the case/the cases* = Fr. *le cas/les cas* —but as terms in a number system *singular* and *plural* correspond formally at least to the extent that in both languages it is the term *plural* which is generally regarded as morphologically marked.

In translation, however, it quite frequently happens that this formal correspondence is departed from, i.e. where the translation equivalent of English *singular* is French *plural* and vice-versa.

e.g.	advice	= des conseils
	news	= des nouvelles
	lightning	= des éclairs
	applause	= des applaudissements
	trousers	= le pantalon
	the dishes	= la vaisselle
	the contents	= le contenu etc.[6]

Again, we might regard English and French as having formally

[6] cf. Vinay et Darbelnet, pp. 119–23.

corresponding systems of deictics, particularly *articles*; each may be said to have four articles, *zero, definite, indefinite* and *partitive*. It is tempting, then, to set up a formal correspondence between the terms of the systems as in this table:

	French	English
Zero	—	—
Definite	le, la, l', les	the
Indefinite	un, une	a, an
Partitive	du, de la, de l', des	some, any

In translation, however, it sometimes happens that the equivalent of an article is not the formally corresponding term in the system:

e.g.

Il est—professeur.	He is *a* teacher.
Il a *la* jambe cassée.	He has *a* broken leg.
*L'*amour	Love
Du vin	Wine

In the following table we give the translation-equivalents of French articles found in French texts with English translations. The number of cases in which a French article has an English equivalent at word-rank is 6958, and the figures given here are percentages; the figure 64·6 against *le* for instance, means that the French definite article (le, la, l', les) has the English definite article as its translation equivalent in 64·6% of its occurrences[7]. By dividing each percentage by 100 we have equivalence-probabilities—thus we may say that, within the limitations stated above, French *le*, etc., will have Eng. *the* as its translation equivalent with probability ·65.

French		English			
	zero	the	some	a	(other)
zero	**67·7**	6·1	0·3	11·2	4·6
le	14·2	**64·6**	—	2·4	18·9
du	**51·3**	9·5	11·0	5·9	22·4
un	6·7	5·8	2·2	**70·2**	15·1

[7] I am indebted to Dr. R. Huddleston for this information.

It is clear from this table that translation equivalence does not entirely match formal correspondence. The most striking divergence is in the case of the French partitive article, *du*, the most frequent equivalent of which is *zero* and not *some*. This casts doubt on the advisability of setting up *any* formal correspondence between the particular terms of the English and French article-systems.

13

Language Varieties in Translation

THE concept of a 'whole language' is so vast and heterogeneous that it is not operationally useful for many linguistic purposes, descriptive, comparative and pedagogical. It is, therefore, desirable to have a framework of categories for the classification of 'sub-languages', or *varieties* within a total language; that is, *idiolects, dialects, registers, styles* and *modes*.

13.1 In theory, a 'whole language' may be described in terms of a vast inventory of grammatical, lexical, phonological and, in some cases, graphological forms, together with information about relevant substance (e.g. features of phonic substance utilized in the phonology), and statistical information (on relative frequency of forms, etc.).[1] All of these may be said to constitute *features* of the language.

Within this theoretical total inventory of features we can establish sub-groupings or *sub-sets* of features. Such sub-sets might be made up more or less at random—for example a sub-set of English items like the following:

arthropoda, ashet, bedight, caitiff, cannot, can't, outwith, triploblastic.

All the items in this sub-set are 'English' in the sense that all may be found in English texts. On the other hand, it is difficult to see much value in a grouping such as this—except for the specific purpose of illustration, as here, or perhaps as an examination-item (as a test of the candidate's ability to recognize varieties of English).

13.11 For most linguistic purposes it is desirable to establish sub-sets of 'features' characteristic of varieties of the language which regularly correlate with certain broad contextual or situational categories. It is clear that the items listed above can be grouped in such a way. *Arthropoda* and *triploblastic* are charac-

---

[1] Whether this 'inventory' is, indeed, an inventory or systematic listing (as in 'taxonomic' description) or an ordered set of rules (as in 'transformational' description) is irrelevant. In either case the description is unmanageably vast.

teristic of scientific, specifically zoological, English. *Ashet* and *outwith* are characteristically Scottish—they occur in texts written or spoken by Scotsmen. *Bedight* and *caitiff* are archaic—they are most characteristically found in texts written a few centuries ago. For many users of English *cannot* is characteristically a written rather than a spoken form. The form *can't* may also occur in written texts, but it differs from *cannot* in that it correlates with situations in which there is a greater degree of familiarity between the writer and his reader(s).

13.2   A *language variety*, then, is a sub-set of formal and/or substantial features which correlates with a particular type of socio-situational feature. For a general classification of varieties we confine ourselves to a consideration of situational correlates which are *constants* in language-situations. These *constants* are (i) the *performer* (speaker or writer), (ii) the *addressee* (hearer or reader), and (iii) the *medium* (phonology or graphology) in which the text is presented.

These three are 'constants' in the sense that they are invariably present, or implied, in all language-situations. Performer and addressee are socio-linguistic *rôles*—whether or not both rôles are played by different individuals is quite irrelevant. A man may talk to himself, in which case he is simultaneously filling the rôles of performer and addressee; or a broadcaster may talk into a 'dead' microphone, unaware that a breakdown has occurred, in which case there are no listeners to fill the rôle of addressee, but the addressee-rôle is still implicit in the performer's selection of language-material. Finally, every text is externalized in some form or other—the performer must always select one or other medium in which to expound the grammatical/lexical forms he is using.

Varieties fall into two major classes: (i) those which are more or less *permanent* for a given performer or group of performers, and (ii) those which are more or less *transient* in that they change with changes in the immediate situation of utterance. The major varieties are listed in 13.21, and discussed in more detail in 13.4 onwards.

13.21   Types of variety related to permanent characteristics of the performer(s).

13.211   *Idiolect:* language variety related to the personal identity of the performer.

13.212   *Dialect:* language variety related to the performer's provenance or affiliations in a geographical, temporal or social dimension.

(i) *Dialect (proper)* or *Geographical Dialect:* variety related to the geographical provenance of the performer: e.g. 'American English', 'British English', 'Scottish English', 'Scots Dialect'.

(ii) *État de langue* or *Temporal Dialect:* variety related to the provenance of the performer, or of the text he has produced, in the time dimension: e.g. 'Contemporary English', 'Elizabethan English', 'Middle English'.

(iii) *Social Dialect:* variety related to the social class or status of the performer: e.g. 'U and non-U'.

13.22   Types of variety related to 'transient' characteristics of the performer and addressee—i.e. related to the immediate situation of utterance.

13.221   *Register:* variety related to the wider social rôle being played by the performer at the moment of utterance: e.g. 'scientific', 'religious', 'civil-service', etc.

13.222   *Style:* variety related to the number and nature of addressees and the performer's relation to them: e.g. 'formal', 'colloquial', 'intimate'.

13.223   *Mode:* variety related to the medium in which the performer is operating: 'spoken', 'written'.

13.23   It would, no doubt, be possible to add to this list of variety-types, particularly by sub-division or conflation. For instance, a more delicate classification of medium-manifestation might supply 'secondary modes'—such as 'telegraphese', a sub-type of the written mode. Again, a kind of conflation might provide us with a 'poetic genre' as a super-variety characterized by potential use of features appropriate to all varieties. For the present study, however, we confine ourselves to the varieties listed here.

13.3   All languages may be presumed to be describable in terms of a number of varieties, though the number and nature of these varies from one language to another—a fact of importance in connection with translation.

All the varieties of a language have features in common—these constitute a *common core* of e.g. grammatical, lexical and phonological forms. In addition to the common core, however, every variety has features which are peculiar to it, and which serve as formal (and sometimes substantial) criteria or *markers* of the variety in question.

The markers of particular varieties may be at any level: phonetic, phonological, graphological, grammatical, lexical. As far as *dialect* is concerned, many languages have a 'standard' or 'literary' dialect, which shows little variation (in its written form at least) from one locality to another. It is convenient, particularly in connection with translation, to regard such a dialect as *unmarked*.

13.4 An *idiolect* is the language variety used by a particular individual. The *markers* of an idiolect may include idiosyncratic statistical features, such as a tendency to exceptionally frequent use of particular lexical items. A person's idiolect may change in detail from day to day (e.g. by the adoption of 'new pronunciations', the acquisition of new lexical items, etc.), and may change extensively in a life-time. For most purposes, however, we may regard an adult's idiolect as relatively static.

It is not always necessary to attempt to translate idiolects: i.e. the personal identity of the performer is not always an important feature of the situation. It may happen, however, that the performer's identity *is* relevant. For instance, in a novel, idiolectal features in the dialogue of one character may be worked into the plot; other characters may remark on these, and they may partly serve to identify the character. In such a case the translator may provide the same character in his translation with an 'equivalent' idiolectal feature[2].

13.5 A *dialect*, as we have seen, is a language variety, marked by formal and/or substantial features relatable to the provenance of a performer or group of performers in one of the three dimensions—space, time and social class.

---

[2] Those features of what is often called the individual 'style' of a particular author are idiolectal, and in a literary translation some attempt may have to be made to find TL equivalents for them. Unusual collocations may also sometimes be regarded as idiolectal—for an example see 14.52.

13.51 *Geographical dialects* may be defined with greater or lesser specificity; thus among dialects of English, for instance, we may for some purposes distinguish between *British English, American English, Australian English*, etc.—such broad, inclusive, dialects being formally distinguished from one another by relatively few markers. For other purposes we may specify sub-varieties within these broad categories, e.g. *Scots English*, and within this, again, still more strictly localized varieties. Similarly, *états de langue* may be arbitrarily marked off along the time-dimension very broadly, as Old English, Middle English, Modern English, etc., or more strictly located within these broad periods, e.g. 19th Century English . . .

13.52 Dialects may present translation problems. As we have said in 13.3 above for most major languages there is a 'standard' or 'literary' dialect which may be regarded as unmarked. Texts in the unmarked dialect of the SL can usually be translated in an equivalent unmarked TL dialect. When the TL has no equivalent unmarked dialect the translator may have to select one particular TL dialect, create a new 'literary' dialect of the TL, or resort to other expedients. This problem not infrequently arises in the translation of the Bible into pre-literate languages, and has been discussed at some length by E. A. Nida[3].

13.53 When an SL text contains passages in a dialect other than the unmarked dialect (e.g. in the dialogue of novels) the translator may have to select an *equivalent* TL dialect. Translation equivalence, as we have seen in 7.4 above, depends on relationship of SL and TL text to 'the same' substance; for total translation, this is situation substance. In the selection of an equivalent TL geographical dialect this means selection of a dialect related to 'the same part of the country' in a geographical sense. Geography is concerned with more than topography and spatial co-ordinates—and human geography is more relevant here than mere location. Thus, in relation to the dialects of Britain, *Cockney* is a *south-eastern* dialect. In translating Cockney dialogue into French, however, most translators would select *Parigot* as the TL equivalent dialect, even though this is a northerly dialect of

[3] *Bible Translating*, Chapter 3.

French. The criterion here is the 'human' or 'social' geographical one of 'dialect of the metropolis' rather than a purely locational criterion.

13.54 The *markers* of the SL dialect may be formally quite different from those of the equivalent TL dialect. There are certainly Cockney markers at all levels, but in many literary texts, Cockney is marked chiefly by phonological features, reflected in such graphological forms as *'alf* or *'arf* for 'half', *wiv* for 'with', and a few grammatical features such as *aint* for 'isn't/ aren't'. In addition there are often *pseudo-phonological* features, indicated by graphological peculiarities such as *orful* for 'awful' and *ter* for 'to'. These graphological forms can be interpreted phonologically only in perfectly normal 'standard' English ways —they are the markers of a purely visual, literary, dialect.

The markers of *Parigot* may include a few graphological/ phonological features, but are likely to be largely at the lexical level, in the form of extensive use of *argot*. This illustrates another case, like those cited in 7.6 above, where phonological/graphological features *appear* to have translation equivalents at the level of lexis; but, as in those examples, this is an illusion. If the translation equivalent of *'e's gorn* is *il a foutu l'camp* this does not mean that lexical items are here translation equivalents of phonological features. The translation equivalence is set up between *varieties* (specifically *Cockney* and *Parigot*): of which the SL *markers* are phonological, and the TL *markers* are lexical; there is no equivalence between phonological and lexical features as such.

13.55 Temporal dialects, or *états de langue*, may also present translation problems. A contemporary *état de langue* of the SL may normally be regarded as *unmarked*, only archaic varieties being marked. In *spoken-spoken* translation[4] both SL and TL texts are normally 'contemporary' or 'unmarked' dialects in the time-dimension. An archaic SL text, however, raises the problem of

---

[4] Here we imply a categorization of 'external' aspects of translation not dealt with in the present essay. For this categorization at least *four* dimensions have to be considered; viz. those of *media* (SL spoken/written, TL spoken/written), *time-relation* (simultaneous/successive), *agent* (human/machine), and for human translation at least, *direction* (L_1 to L_2, or L_2 to L_1).

whether, and how, the translator should seek to select an equivalent archaic TL text. Here, as in the case of geographical dialect, equivalence of absolute location in time is normally neither possible nor desirable. The 12th Century Russian *Slovo o polku Igoreve*, for example, would not normally be translated into 12th Century English; in this form it would be considerably less intelligible to a contemporary English reader than the original is to a contemporary Russian. Dennis Ward[5] in his article on translation of the Slovo has argued against archaism in the TL text, with the exception of his deliberate selection of *host* as translation equivalent of the lexical item *polk*. Nevertheless, parts of his brilliant translation have a somewhat 'archaic flavour'— the markers here being *lexical items* such as *girded, beasts, warriors, behold*, the use of *brothers* as a term of address, not to mention lexical items which are of low frequency in contemporary English texts because their contextual meanings relate to archaic objects or institutions such as *bows, quivers, shields, pennons, gerfalcon, pagan hosts*; occasional features of clause-structure; phonological features of alliteration and metre (successful partial phonological translations) and so on. Such features are for the English reader, markers of a slightly archaic *état de langue*, appropriate to the subject as well as being to some extent a translation equivalent of the SL *état de langue*.

13.6   *Register*, *Style* and *Mode* are language varieties related to the immediate situation of utterance.

13.61   By *register* we mean a variety correlated with the performer's *social rôle* on a given occasion. Every normal adult plays a series of different social rôles—one man, for example, may function at different times as head of a family, motorist, cricketer, member of a religious group, professor of biochemistry and so on, and within his idiolect he has varieties (shared by other persons and other idiolects) appropriate to these rôles. When the professor's wife tells him to 'stop talking like a professor' she is protesting at a misuse of register.

13.611   Registers, like dialects, can be defined with lesser or

---

[5] 'On translating *Slovo o polku Igoreve*', *The Slavonic Review*. The translation itself 'The Tale of the Host of Igor . . .' appeared as a supplement to Ward's paper to the IVth International Congress of Slavists, Moscow 1958.

greater specificity; thus, while in English we may identify a general *scientific* register, we may also differentiate sub-registers within this. Register-*markers* are chiefly *lexical* (most obviously 'technical terms', but including other items), and *grammatical*, particularly grammatical-statistical features such as the high frequency (30% to 50%) of *passive* verb forms, and the low frequency of the pronouns *I you he* and *she* in English scientific register.

13.612 In translation, the selection of an appropriate register in the TL is often important. Here, if the TL has no equivalent register, untranslatability may result. One of the problems of translating scientific texts into certain languages which have recently become National Languages, such as Hindi, is that of finding, or creating, an equivalent scientific register. And here again, the *equivalence* is between *varieties*; an English scientific text may have, inter alia, a relatively high percentage occurrence of *passives*; its Russian translation a relatively high percentage occurrence of *javlaets'a + instrumental*. The Russian *javlaets'a* is not necessarily the translation equivalent of an English passive; both are merely *markers* of *equivalent registers*.

13.62 By *style* we mean a variety which correlates with the number and nature of the addressees and the performer's relationship to them. Styles vary along a scale which may be roughly characterized as *formal . . . informal*. For English, Martin Joos has suggested five styles: *frozen, formal, consultative, casual* and *intimate*[6].

The markers of styles may be lexical, grammatical or phonological. Not much is known in detail about English styles, though it is probably true, as Joos points out, that ellipsis is one marker of *casual* style: e.g. *Coffee's cold. Bought it yesterday. Leaving?*— another is the use of slang. For English we can probably regard *consultative* style as the unmarked style in the spoken mode, though *formal* style may be the unmarked style in the written mode.

As with registers, so with styles, translatability depends on the existence of an equivalent style in the TL. In English, style-

[6] 'The Isolation of Styles', *Georgetown Monographs on Languages and Linguistics* 12 (1959), pp. 107–13.

markers tend to be dispersed over a number of levels of the language, including lexis and phonology. In many languages, particularly in South East Asia, the translation equivalents of particular English styles may be more rigidly built into grammar and lexis—as the use of specifically 'self-abasing' or 'honorific' terms in a system of pronouns, or similar obligatory alternative items in lexical sets.

Here again, however, translation equivalence must be set up between the varieties as such, and the specific markers may be very different in the SL and TL texts. Moreover, the equivalence is ultimately based on similarities of situation-substance—only, those which are stylistically relevant in one language may not be in another. An English youth may easily address his father in casual style; an oriental youth on the other hand may have to use honorific forms in such a situation. Both *respect* and *affection* may be present in the situation, but respect may not be a stylistically relevant feature for the English son, while it *is* relevant for the Asian son.

This is one reason for divergences here, as elsewhere, between formal-correspondence and translation equivalence. Two languages might possess a roughly corresponding set of styles; but cultural factors may dictate the use of a non-corresponding style as translation equivalent.

13.7 It should be noted that there may be syncretisms and incompatibilities between varieties. For one thing, in English, as we move 'down' the style-scale from *formal* to *casual* the *registral* differences become less marked. A professor of zoology may give a lecture to a learned society in zoological register and formal style. He may continue to use zoological register with the consultative style he uses in a seminar with graduate students, or with the casual style he uses in common-room scientific gossip with colleagues. Specific lexical items—the 'technical terms' of zoology—will still be there as register-markers in his casual style, but most of the other markers of scientific register—the less specifically zoological, but still scientific, lexical items, the grammatical markers and so on—will have disappeared.

There may be incompatibility between, say, a rural dialect and scientific register, or between casual style and religious register and so on. Such incompatibilities may have an effect on translation. Thus some Hindi translations of English novels and short stories show no attempt to use a particular Hindi 'marked dialect' as translation equivalent of rural (geographical) dialect or 'uneducated' social dialect in English dialogue. It is possible that this reflects a dialect/mode incompatibility in Hindi—i.e. the non-compatibility of 'sub-standard' Hindi dialect with the written mode.

In many cases a change of style or register involves a corresponding change of dialect or even language. In Arabic, for example, the Classical dialect is hardly compatible with casual style. Many Indians will switch from, say, Hindi or Marathi to English whenever they speak or write about scientific subjects; such people have no scientific register in their 'mother tongue', but only in English.

14

The Limits of Translatability

14.1   In 7.6 above we were able to state certain absolute limits of translatability, namely: translation between media is impossible, and translation between the medium-levels and the levels of grammar/lexis is likewise impossible. These absolute limitations derive directly from our theory of translation equivalence. For translation equivalence to occur, SL and TL items must be relatable to (at least some of) the same features of substance, and it is easy to see that there is an absolute absence of similarity between phonic and graphic substance, and between either of these and situation substance.

14.11   The limits of translatability in total translation are, however, much more difficult to state. Indeed, translatability here appears, intuitively, to be a *cline* rather than a clear-cut dichotomy. SL texts and items are *more* or *less* translatable rather than absolutely *translatable* or *untranslatable*. In total translation, translation equivalence depends on the interchangeability of the SL and TL text in the same situation—ultimately, that is, on relationship of SL and TL texts to (at least some of) the same relevant features of situation-substance.

14.12   At this point we must consider more closely the term *relevant*. In Chapter 7 we talked about *linguistically relevant* features of situation (substance)—those features, or bundles of features, which led to the performer selecting this or that item of his language. Similarly, in the example in 5.4 we saw that for a Russian speaker, the sex of the performer was linguistically relevant, that is, led to selection of the form *prišla* as opposed to *prišel*. For the equivalent English text the sex of the performer was linguistically irrelevant—i.e. did not lead to selection of one particular linguistic form rather than another.

The English and Russian texts, *I've arrived* and *ja prišla* operate perfectly well as translation equivalents in spite of this difference, because the sex of the performer though linguistically relevant for the Russian text is not relevant to the communicative function of the text in that situation; in other words, the Russian performer is obliged by a formal feature of her language to make this incidental reference to her sex, even though this is not 'what she intends to say'.

14.13   We can distinguish, then, between situational features which are *linguistically relevant*, and those which are *functionally relevant* in that they are relevant to the communicative function of the text in that situation. For translation equivalence to occur, then, both SL and TL text must be relatable to the *functionally* relevant features of the situation. A decision, in any particular case, as to what is functionally relevant in this sense must in our present state of knowledge remain to some extent a matter of opinion. The total co-text will supply information which the translator will use in coming to a decision, but it is difficult to define functional relevance in general terms.

14.14   Translation fails—or untranslatability occurs—when it is impossible to build functionally relevant features of the situation into the contextual meaning of the TL text. Broadly speaking, the cases where this happens fall into two categories. Those where the difficulty is *linguistic*, and those where it is *cultural*.

14.2   In *linguistic untranslatability* the functionally relevant features include some which are in fact formal features of the *language* of the SL text. If the TL has no formally corresponding feature, the text, or the item, is (relatively) untranslatable.

Linguistic untranslatability occurs typically in cases where an *ambiguity* peculiar to the SL text is a functionally relevant feature —e.g. in SL puns. *calembour   -jeux de mots:*

14.21   Ambiguities arise from two main sources, (i) *shared exponence* of two or more SL grammatical or lexical items, (ii) *polysemy* of an SL item with no corresponding TL polysemy.

14.211   By *shared exponence* we mean those cases where two or more distinct grammatical or lexical items are expounded in one and the same phonological or graphological form.

A grammatical example in English is the shared exponence of the two distinct morphemes '(Nominal) plural' and '(Verbal) third person singular present' both of which are frequently expounded graphologically by -*s*, as in *cats* and *eats*. In most cases, there is no ambiguity, since the co-text (as here) indicates clearly which item is being expounded, and the translation equivalent is then not in doubt. But cases of ambiguity can arise, an example is *Time flies*. If this piece of text occurred in a normal conversation there would be no translation problem; the co-text would show whether the contextual meaning was 'How quickly time passes'. or something like 'Make observations on the speed of flies', and the appropriate translation equivalent would be obvious. But when the whole point of the text is to provide an example of ambiguity, as it is in this paragraph, then translation is virtually impossible. The ambiguity itself (a feature of the English language —the SL) is a functionally relevant feature of the situation.

A lexical example might be *bank*, which is the graphological exponent of two distinct lexical items in English.[1] This normally presents no problem in translation; the co-text normally shows whether, for example, the French translation equivalent should be *banque* or *rive*. But *bank* is untranslatable when the ambiguity is itself a functionally relevant feature, as in Ogden and Richard's punning fable about Amoeba[2], which begins:

'Realize thyself, Amoeba dear', said Will; and Amoeba realized herself, and there was no Small Change but many Checks on the Bank wherein the wild Time grew and grew and grew.'

Here it is clear that the reader is expected to relate the graphological form *Bank* to *both* the lexical items which it expounds. This is impossible in French, where the translation equivalent must be either *banque* or *rive* and not both at once; and other untranslatable ambiguities are equally obvious in this text.

14.212   The second type of linguistic ambiguity is due to what would usually be called *polysemy*; that is, not to the fact that two or more items have the same exponent, but that one single item has more than one meaning. Strictly speaking, the term polysemy

---

[1] That *bank* represents two items—not just 'one item with two meanings'— is intuitively felt by English speakers. The formal confirmation of this intuition will no doubt be forthcoming when computers have demonstrated that 'bank' occurs in two slightly overlapping but largely quite distinct collocational ranges.

[2] C. K. Ogden and I. A. Richards, *The Meaning of Meaning*, Appendix E.

is misleading. It is not a case of one item having several meanings, but of one item having a wide or general contextual meaning, covering a wide range of specific situational features. In any given situation, only one out of this wide range of potentially, or linguistically, relevant features is functionally relevant. An example is the Russian *s verxu* the contextual meaning of which can be roughly summarized in English as being 'from or off a higher position'. *S verxu* is thus appropriate to situations in which the English translation equivalent would be 'from above', 'from upstairs', 'from upriver' . . . etc. Normally, the co-text shows which part of the total contextual meaning of *s verxu* is functionally relevant, and translation presents no problem. But on rare occasions the linguistic feature itself, the wideness of meaning of the item *s verxu*—its polysemy—is a functionally relevant feature. In this case, translation is virtually impossible—an example is given in 14.31 below.

14.22   In addition to *ambiguity*, due to shared exponence or to polysemy, another kind of linguistic untranslatability can occur. In this case it is not *polysemy*, but rather what might be called *oligosemy* which is the cause.

If an SL item has a particularly restricted range of meaning it may not be possible to match this restriction in the TL. Normally, again, this does not matter. The Russian *prišla*, as we saw above, means 'came' or 'arrived' *on foot*. English has no lexical item with a correspondingly restricted range of contextual meaning; but this does not prevent English *came* or *arrived* from often being a perfect translation equivalent. In special cases, however, this restriction of meaning—the 'oligosemy' of *prišla* as opposed to English *came*—may itself be a functionally relevant feature of the situation. This, like the previous type of ambiguity, is illustrated in 14.3 below.

14.3   Examples of (relative) linguistic untranslatability due to all the factors dealt with above are well illustrated in the following passage in Maxim Gorki's *Childhood*.

14.31   The child, Gorki, has been ill in bed for some time. His grandmother has travelled down the Volga from Nijni Novgorod to look after the family. To the little boy, she is just a new grown-up who has suddenly appeared on the scene. The following conversation occurs, presented here with a rank-bound (largely word-word, partly morpheme-morpheme) and unbounded translation.

Ty otkuda prišla.
Thou whence came-on-foot?
Where have you come from?

S verxu, iz Nižnego, da ne prišla,
From above, from Lower and not came-on-foot.
From upriver/upstairs, from Nijni/lower, and I didn't come on foot.

Po vode-to ne xod'at.
On water-(!) not they-go-on-foot.
You don't walk on water!

The child finds this funny and confusing; he reflects on who lives upstairs and downstairs in the house, and he wonders how one can come down the stairs without going on foot; and what has water to do with it?

14.32 The untranslatability of this text, or rather of certain items in it, has nothing to do with cultural differences in the wider sense; it is purely linguistic. It rests on the SL items *prišla*, *s verxu*, *Nižnego*, and these illustrate all three of the causes of linguistic untranslatability referred to above.

14.321 *Nižnego* illustrates ambiguity arising from shared exponence—*nižnij* (genitive singular *nižnego*) as exponent of (*a*) an adjective meaning *lower* and (*b*) the common abbreviation of the place-name Nijni Novgorod ('Lower Newtown'). This is virtually untranslatable into English because a comparable shared exponence does not occur—*Lower* may occur as a place-name *element*, but it is not normally used by itself as an abbreviation. *S verxu* is an example of ambiguity due to 'polysemy' or the wide range of contextual meaning of this item. Out of the total range of situational features with the general characteristic of being 'from above', the child selects the specific feature 'from above in the house', or 'from upstairs', while the grandmother means 'from up yonder', or 'from upriver'. English cannot easily combine these specific features in the contextual meaning of one lexical item; it must select 'from upstairs', or 'from up yonder', or 'from upriver'. The equivalent 'from above' would be collocationally strange in this text. Finally, *prišla* illustrates a case of 'oligosemy'. The item *prišla* means 'came' or 'have come' *on foot*. In many situations, the situational feature referred to by 'on foot' is not functionally relevant, though it is linguistically relevant for Russian. Consequently, a perfectly good English translation can often ignore this feature and use the English *come* which has a wider situational range. In this example, however, this feature, which is linguistically relevant for Russian, is also functionally relevant, since it is an important factor in causing the child's bewilderment.

14.322   We might attempt a more 'faithful' translation somewhat on these lines:

Where have you walked in from?
I've just come down—from Lower.
And I didn't walk. You don't walk on water.

It is clear, however, that this translation is unsatisfactory. The sentence 'Where have you walked in from?' is out of register. 'From Lower' would convey nothing to an English reader without a footnote explaining that 'Lower' is a translation of the abbreviated form of Nijni Novgorod. And, finally, 'I've just come down' (or any obvious alternative) does not suggest the quite specific interpretation 'from upstairs' which the child Gorki gives to the Russian *s verxu*.

14.4   The 'untranslatability' exemplified in the last few paragraphs is called linguistic untranslatability because failure to find a TL equivalent is due entirely to differences between the source *language* and the target *language*. Such differences are, of course, the rule rather than the exception, since formal correspondence is exceedingly rare—but formal differences between languages do not normally preclude the finding of translation equivalents. Formal linguistic differences—differences between the SL and the TL organization of situation-substance—lead to translation failure only when the SL formal feature is *itself* a textually-functionally-relevant feature. The related situational features may themselves be perfectly commonplace in both the SL and TL cultures.

What appears to be a quite different problem arises, however, when a situational feature, functionally relevant for the SL text, is completely *absent* from the culture of which the TL is a part. This may lead to what we have called *cultural untranslatability*. This type of untranslatability is usually less 'absolute' than linguistic untranslatability.

14.41 We have already referred in passing to a Finnish lexical item which may be untranslatable into English—namely *sauna* (see 6.31 above). There may be texts in which *bath* or *bathhouse* would be an adequate translation equivalent. But the Finnish and the English institutions are certainly different, and a sauna is not always a separate building—it may be a room in a house, hotel, or ship for instance. In this latter case, the obvious English equivalent *bathroom* would probably be evaluated by any translator as inappropriate.

It is a curious fact that the Japanese lexical item *huro(-ba)* seems to be more easily translatable as *bath* or *bathroom* than the Finnish *sauna*. And yet the Japanese bath(room) is in some respects as different from an English bath(room) as is the sauna—and both of the non-English institutions have non-English features in common.

As distinct from the English bath, which is normally a solitary activity, the Finnish and Japanese baths are, or may often be, communal. The Finnish and Japanese 'bathrooms' are, each in its own way, quite differently constructed and furnished from an English bathroom.

The sauna, however, differs still more (has more non-English situational features) from the English bath or bathroom; it involves neither immersion in hot water, nor washing the body (which is done outside the sauna and is not an integral part of 'taking a sauna'). The Japanese institution, like the English one, does involve immersion in hot water, and washing the body is an integral part of the bath-taking and is performed inside the bathroom itself, though before actually entering the water to soak.

It looks, therefore, as if equivalence of material aspects of the institution are less important than equivalence in its major personal or social function (washing the body and soaking in hot water) in promoting translatability. This reminds us of the point referred to in 13.53 above where it was suggested that the human or socio-geographical status of a SL dialect might be the essential situational feature determining the selection of an equivalent TL dialect, rather than its geographical location.

14.42   Articles of clothing provide other examples of features of material culture which differ from one culture to another and may lead to translation difficulties. The contextual meaning of the Japanese lexical item *yukata*, for example, includes some such features as 'loose robe bound by a sash, worn by either men or women, supplied to guests in a Japanese inn or hotel, worn in the evening indoors or out of doors in street or café, worn in bed . . .' etc. Parts of this total range are covered by such English lexical items as *dressing-gown, bath-robe, house-coat, pyjamas, night-gown . . .* etc., and in some texts the relevant situational features might be just those common to both *dressing-gown* and *yukata* on that particular occasion. But no English item is relatable to the full range of situational features, and there are likely to be texts where no possible English translation equivalent exists. No English garment, for instance, is worn both in bed and in the street (except in emergencies) and certainly no garment is supplied by English hotels to their guests.

The solution adopted by most translators here would be to transfer the SL item *yukata* into the TL text, leaving its contextual meaning to emerge from the co-text (or else explaining it in a footnote). Another possibility would be to use the item *kimono* as translation equivalent, since this originally Japanese lexical item is already 'naturalized' as a loan-word in English, though *yukata* and *kimono* do not mean the same in Japanese.

14.43   It is often supposed that certain more 'abstract' lexical items such as *home* or *democracy* are relatively untranslatable. This is largely an illusion. There is no doubt that such English texts as *He's at home* or *I'm going home* can readily be provided with translation equivalents in most languages. It is only rarely that the functionally relevant situational features related to *home* include that nebulous sentimentality which is supposed not to be related to lexical items in other languages—e.g. perhaps in the song *Home, Sweet Home*.

As for *democracy*, this is in any case an international term—

which means essentially that it is untranslatable because it often need not *be* translated—since it is already present in the lexis of many languages; an 'international term' being a lexical item with recognizably similar phonological/graphological exponents in several languages, and having a common contextual meaning. The total *range* of situational features relatable to the contextual meaning of *democracy* includes features which are present in some national and political situations but absent from others—the co-text generally guides the reader to selection of the appropriate situational features in any particular case. Even within one and the same language, *democracy* may be relatable to some different situational features in the registers of different political parties.

14.5   Although we have, following a somewhat obvious and intuitive approach, distinguished between linguistic and cultural untranslatability it may be questioned whether such a distinction is ultimately necessary. In many cases, at least, what renders 'culturally untranslatable' items 'untranslatable' is the fact that the use in the TL text of any *approximate* translation equivalent produces an *unusual collocation* in the TL. To talk of 'cultural untranslatability' may be just another way of talking about collocational untranslatability: the impossibility of finding an equivalent collocation in the TL. And this would be a type of linguistic untranslatability.

We might define collocational untranslatability thus: untranslatability arising from the fact that any possible TL near-equivalent of a given SL lexical item has a low probability of collocation with TL equivalents of items in the SL text which collocate normally with the given SL item.

14.51   Thus, in the Japanese text *hoteru-no yukata*, the item *hoteru-no* has the straightforward English translation equivalent *hotel's* or *hotel* (as modifier); but any possible English near-equivalent of yukata would collocate strangely with *hotel*—i.e. *hotel dressing-gown, hotel bath-robe, hotel nightgown*, etc., are all low probability collocations in English—though the original Japanese collocation is a normal, or high-probability one.

More extended examples will make this point even clearer. The following two texts are imaginary translations from Finnish and Japanese respectively.

101

(i) 'They lay on the hot upper benches of the *bathroom* inhaling the aromatic scent of the birch twigs.'

(ii) 'After his bath he enveloped his still-glowing body in the simple hotel *bath-robe* and went out to join his friends in the café down the street.'

14.511   Both of these would 'read strangely' to an English reader unacquainted with Finnish or Japanese institutions. This strangeness *can* be attributed to the strangeness of the situations they suggest—to the mild 'cultural shock' induced by the image of (i) people (more than one) lying about on hot benches in a birch-scented bathroom and (ii) of a *hotel* bath-robe which, moreover, is worn in the street. We *can*, in other words, say that *bathroom* and *bath-robe* are bad translations, and if *no* other English lexical items, less suprising in these co-texts, can be found—then we may say that the SL items *sauna* and *yukata* are untranslatable —for cultural reasons.

14.512   But we can also describe the strange effect produced by these translations not as 'cultural shock' but as 'collocational shock'. In other words we can attribute the relative untranslatability of the two SL items to a purely formal linguistic feature— unusualness of collocation. In theory, this could be done without any appeal at all to the contextual meanings of the texts—and hence without any reference to cultural differences. If a sufficient amount of information were available on the collocation of lexical items in any pair of SL and TL languages the ability to identify such so-called 'culturally untranslatable' items might, in theory, be programmed into a computer for the purposes of machine translation.

14.52   The case is different with the following (genuine) translation from French. The SL text is a sentence from 'La Chatte', by Colette[3]. The English TL text reads:

> '*The sun kindles a crackling of birds in the gardens.*'

There are certainly strange, or low-probability, collocations here. But in this case the strangeness of the collocations is not due to 'untranslatability'—on the contrary, it is, indeed, an indication

[3] This example is taken from the essay on translation in J. G. Weightman, *On Language and Writing* (Sylvan Press, 1947).

of a 'good' translation, because a very similar strangeness of collocations exists in the original:

'Le soleil allume un crépitement d'oiseaux dans les jardins.'

In other words, the collocation *soleil—allume—crépitement—oiseaux* is about as unusual as the collocation: *sun—kindles—crackling—birds.* From this we may deduce that collocational *abnormality* in the TL text is a symptom of (so-called 'cultural') untranslatability only when the original SL text is collocationally *normal.* When the SL text is itself collocationally abnormal an equivalent collocational abnormality in the TL text may be merely the mark of a 'good' translation.

In this particular example from Colette there is, as Weightman points out, some degree of untranslatability. The French item *crépitement* has certain associations for a French reader which are —perhaps inevitably—lost in the English translation. The major untranslatable 'association' of *crépitement* is that it is somewhat reminiscent of *pépiement*, a lexical item used to refer to the twittering of birds. Now this untranslatable association of *crépitement* is a good example of one of the types of linguistic untranslatability referred to in 14.211 above, namely *shared exponence.* The phonological forms represented graphologically by *crépitement* and *pépiement* are partially alike—in other words, we have here two French lexical items with (partially) shared exponence. Whether or not we regard the resultant simultaneous reference to situational features of the contextual meanings of both these items as functionally relevant or not may be a matter of opinion. But if we do accept this view, and if we do in consequence say that *crépitement* is to some degree untranslatable, then we must accept the fact that this is a case of *linguistic* untranslatability.

14.6   Here we have been able only to touch on the problem of the limits of translatability. The subject is a large one and requires much further study. If, indeed, it should turn out that 'cultural untranslatability' is ultimately describable in all cases as a variety of *linguistic* untranslatability, then the power of translation-theory will have been considerably increased and, among other things, the horizon of machine translation will have been enlarged.

559294

P 306.C33
ledl,circ
A linguistic theory of translation

C.1

3 1862 002 338 362
University of Windsor Libraries

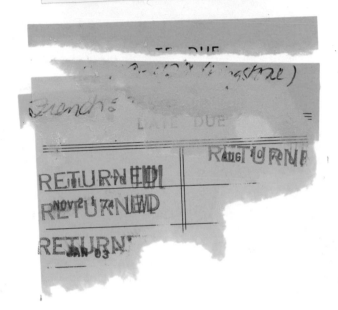

R